Valleys and Mountains

Navigating ~ A Memoir

MERILEE KAUFMAN

Valleys and Mountains

Copyright © 2024 by Merilee Kaufman

All rights reserved.

Published by Red Penguin Books

Bellerose Village, NY

ISBN

Digital 978-1-63777-550-9

Print 978-1-63777-551-6

No part of this book may be reproduced in any form or by any electronic or mechanical means, including information storage and retrieval systems, without written permission from the author, except for the use of brief quotations in a book review.

*I dedicate this book to you, dear Herb, for without you, there's be no "me."
Well, maybe a little.*

Contents

Chapter 1	1
Chapter 2	17
Chapter 3	24
Chapter 4	31
Chapter 5	42
Chapter 6	46
Chapter 7	53
Chapter 8	58
Chapter 9	65
Chapter 10	72
Chapter 11	78
Chapter 12	82
Chapter 13	93
Chapter 14	104
Chapter 15	121
Postscript	125
Afterword	131
Acknowledgments	133
About the Author	135

One

I, Merilee Dale Sisapel, was born June 24, 1943, at Lenox Hill Hospital and raised in The Bronx, New York. My mom, Sylvia, was a homemaker; my dad, Louis, a policeman. My sister Elaine, was six years older and I called her *Sis* or Sister.

Pre-marriage, Father Louis Sisapel and Mother Sylvia, amble down the Atlantic City boardwalk

Mom told me that she met Dad on a trip with friends to Bear Mountain.

She also told me that Sis, as a kid, read *Terry and the Pirates* comic strip. Sis loved a freckled-faced, pigtailed character named Merrily. And my parents needed an "m", as I was named after my grandmother Malia.

Growing up, Mom, introducing me, would say, "This is our daughter Merilee Dale."

"What an unusual name!" came the almost usual response..

"Not so." Checking out of the hospital, the head nurse told Mom that they had just checked out another newborn baby–this one by the name of Merrily Gale ."

Growing up, introduction after introduction, the story stuck.

I attended PS 94. Mom walked me, lunchbox in hand, to school. As I got a bit older, and more independent, I walked by myself. In a school play, I played *The Proud Princess*. Mom attended the Assembly. My character's costume was a green satin dress, skirt down to the floor, with sparkles.

VALLEYS AND MOUNTAINS

Merilee posing as the Proud Princess outside her apartment building

That's when disaster struck. I had to sing. I began and slowly felt my throat choking. I could not finish and began to cry. To avoid another 'episode,' I did not perform in public, until....

At Junior High School 80, I got good marks but, with classmates, stole midterms. We got a tremendous bawling out from the Assistant Principal, Miss Birnbaum, and a warning that if I ever did such a thing again, a suspension would follow. Miss Birnbaum also chastised me and some friends for wearing sweaters that contoured my newly forming bosom.

I was a member of the Blue Angels club. We had knit blue club sweaters, with three black stripes around the arm. Across the back, the sweaters displayed our Blue Angels name. Members included Marsha, Elaine,

Kathy, Brenda, Diane, Tema and Shelley and we met weekly at the Jewish Center on Tryon Avenue.

Dues collected, the agenda included discussing boys, upcoming dances and what we'd wear. When a school situation arose, we'd tackle that, too.

At JHS 80, my home-room teacher, Mr. Frank Micelotta ("Micey," for all of us) had a deep voice, was tall, thin, with glasses and was very strict. He named me Editor of the yearbook. When I stood close to him for work, I could smell cigarette smoke. He wore a gold wedding band and sometimes shared tidbits of his family life with the homeroom class.

I frequently saw *Micey* talking outside the room of economics teacher Mr. Arnold Moss, eye-glassed and also bald. Friendly colleagues, I told myself.

In my ninth grade, I came to school one morning to learn that Micey was not in the homeroom. He'd killed himself, my fellow students had learned.

By this time, I'd learned about homosexuals, and later, wondered if Micey and Mr. Moss were more than 'just colleagues.'

Sunday mornings, I walked with Dad to Jerome Avenue to pick up rolls and bagels to supplement Mom's breakfasts. One day, on our way home, we stopped at a candy store when Dad told me to phone his precinct. Through the glass window, I heard him say "honey," and reported this to Mom.

When I was about 10, I could walk to *The Avenue* alone. One day, while returning home, on my left, I noticed a man driving a car slowly. Curious, and looking over, I noticed a beige something rolled up in his hands between his legs. I figured it was a beige beret. He slowed the car down further, smiled and waved me over. I took a few steps, then saw it was not a beret, but rather his penis. Horrified at the sight, I turned around and dashed home.

Mom warned me, "If you don't know the driver, stay far away!"

DAD: NEVER MISS PLEASURE

Mom told me that when Dad's younger brother David died on the handball courts, Dad promised that he would never miss any pleasure.

She also told me that, when making love, Dad sounded like an animal.

VACATION

Like most families, we too went on family vacations each year. Most vacations our family spent in Asbury Park, New Jersey. Dad drove us all there and we stayed at Betty's Rooming House. Asbury Park offered things for hobbyists.

My artistic leanings led me to making sea-shell earrings and pins. I'd buy the pins, plastic backs and an assortment of colored seashells and paste them. The pins went on the backs and my designs of the colored shells on the fronts. On the boardwalk I sold some and, on returning home, I gave away many of them as gifts.

I had a boyfriend there named Steven. Brown hair and eyes, he was a little chubby, but he listened to me, and I to him. Sometimes he told me jokes and we both laughed. Together, we fed peanuts to the pigeons.

The boardwalk boasted rides and games. I loved the Cuddle-Up. Flat, when the ride began, the cars would slide around the metal floor plates, gliding fast onto one another, round plate after round plate, again and again. The rapid spin was exciting. The horizontal slides, with cars sharply turning, providing quick jolts, gave me, like other riders, many thrills. We all howled on the quick turns. It was safe for me, or at least that's how Mom felt.

Another vacation spot was the Metropole Hotel in Atlantic City. Dad was a swimmer and decided to teach me to swim. My photos show us in the pool, me, with a smile on my face, sitting on top of Dad's shoulders.

And then there was also the Atlantic City boardwalk arcade. Here, Dad taught me and Sis to shoot the fishes. Electronically powered by our pistol-gripping squeezes, these fake fish, amid colored water rows, swam ahead to the end. Dad won frequently, and me and Sis, some of the time.

ACCIDENT

For one vacation, Dad was driving in the Jersey Turnpike's left lane. A bicycle fell off the car ahead of us. Trying to stop, our car toppled, falling into the lane of the oncoming traffic. Fortunately no cars came at that moment.

"Meri, Elaine, Lou, are you okay?" Mom called out.

"We're okay," me and Sis answered, and "Yes, Syl, I'm okay," said Dad,

"How about you?"

"I'm fine, too," we heard a tremble in Mom's voice.

Though shaken, we were all safe. We also had the good luck of a nearby policeman in a squad car, stopping and assisting us. He righted our car and made sure we were fine.

All okay, happily, we traveled on.

Back home, for Saturday matinees I'd meet my friend Elaine. Before entering the David Marcus Movie Theatre, from a nearby appetizing store, we'd buy and share half a pound of sunflower seeds, and bring these, in their white paper bags, into the theater. Throughout the film, we cracked shells, downed the seeds and spit the shells on the floor.

The matron, a middle aged woman, with gray hair and glasses and a thick foreign accent, in her white uniform, walked the theater aisles. Coming to us, pointing her flashlight to the littered floor, she exclaimed, "Why did you do that? You shouldn't!"

She moved on, returning soon with her sweeper. Elaine and I chuckled softly.

I was afraid to walk in the dark. One November afternoon, the sun was nearly set. Even though she was considerably shorter than I, Elaine would walk the two extra blocks beyond her DeKalb Avenue home to my building on Bainbridge Avenue and say goodbye.

I entered the apartment to find, in the foyer, Dad's closet door open. His shirts, slacks, shoes, socks, jackets, Stetson hat, belts and revolver: gone. All gone.

Mom was on the couch crying. I went to her side, put my arm around her and held her to my chest. Her tears poured onto my shoulder, her sobs onto my chest.

"He was having an affair with that sales lady. My investigation showed that she worked in Macy's Pet Department. I'd previously warned him. However his perfumed shirt with lipstick on the collar was the final straw."

"If you continue, you'd better leave this apartment," she had warned him.

And that's exactly what he did. He left.

Concerned with Mom, I had no time to process what this loss meant to me, and so repressed it.

I had asked Mom how it was giving birth to me.

MOM'S GIVING BIRTH TO ME

"I was all alone. Daddy was on night duty. My sisters didn't come to assist, nor did Uncle Al. Of course, Grandma couldn't come by herself downtown to Lenox Hill Hospital. So I gave birth to you alone.

"Recuperating at the hospital, I walked across the hospital bridge and considered jumping. Then I thought about you and your sister–and decided I couldn't commit my children to foster care. Also, I had to care for Grandma. I decided to live."

Most of my friends had both parents in their home. I grew up–an adolescent with basically one parent–I felt so embarrassed and ashamed.

My sister tried to help. Summer weekends, with her friends, Sis would take me to Orchard Beach, these young women smoking and hunting men.

Studying for the Bar exam, Dad had been busy much of the time. While in the PD, he worked many nights, or so he told us. However, I do remember that some days, he made time to see my performance in Riverdance, a production at nearby Reservoir Oval Park.

In that park, Dad also taught Sister and me to ride a bike.

In the nearby Poe Park one day my sister had told me that Dad had taken her to "visit my friend," he'd said.

According to Sis, sitting on a bench, this lady wore a black suit and black hat with a veil.

"Dorothy," Dad said to the lady, "this is my daughter Elaine."

"Hello, Elaine," said the veiled lady.

My sister told me she acknowledged her but said nothing more.

When I grew up I realized that a black outfit was usually symbolic of the outfit worn by "the other woman."

THE DRINK

About a month after his leaving our home, Dad invited Mom to have a drink at the swanky Sherry Netherlands Hotel on Central Park South.

After small talk, when Dad finished his scotch and soda and Mom, her whisky sour, Dad said to Mom, "If you make any trouble for me–reveal my affair, to the Police Department or The Shomrim Society, of which I'm now president—I'll take my pistol and shoot both you and myself."

Mom thanked Dad for the drink, said goodbye, turned and returned home.

Dad would call and invite me to Thursday night dinners. He'd pick me up in the family's 1953 gray Chevrolet, At the Lido Riviera on Valentine Avenue in The Bronx, he'd order veal parmigiana. I ordered the same. He'd talk, ask me questions about school. Throat choking, I could hardly answer or even speak.

A year or two passed, and now, Dad was doing some work for the Better Business Bureau. After dinner Thursday nights, walking along Fordham Road, Dad told me about his investigations for the BBB.

"This sometimes requires that I go to Staten Island and, at times, it was difficult getting passengers off the Ferry," he told me. I just listened.

Returning from these dinner dates, Mom would inquire: "Did Dad say anything bad about anything, particularly about our separation?" My answer was negative, my chest still churning.

JHS

I enjoyed and did well in Junior High School. Time was near to select a high school.

I had fun acting, and the guidance counselor, Barbara Brown, suggested that The High School of Performing Arts, with their fine drama department, would be an excellent choice.

Miss Brown, dark flowing hair tied back, glasses on her neck, dressed usually in big black flowing skirts and a black sweater, counseled me and helped select a monologue to work on. She chose the Carson McCullough play, *The Member of the Wedding* and I was to play Frankie the adolescent girl, searching for her identity.

We worked together on the lines and my reading.

"Feel the part of Frankie and let your audience see it. And hold your head up, speak loud–be heard!"

By this time, my mom had begun dating a man named Irving.

Irving was very kind. He had a car and would drive Mom and me to the Westchester County Shopping Center, where, in Wanamaker's Department Store, she could shop for shoes to fit her aching feet.

For my dramatic training, Irving told us he had a friend in show business. She lived downtown and her name was Jillian Love. Irving spoke to her and put me in touch.

We agreed upon a date where Mom and I would go down to Miss Love's studio and work on this monologue. Mom and I took the D train down. We entered the Riverside Drive apartment. I was astonished when I saw, in the large room, the wall-to-wall bookcases–chock full.

Miss Love was of medium height and thin, with blonde hair pulled back and large horn-rimmed eyeglasses hanging around her neck. Mom sat on the side and browsed books and magazines.

I read and Miss Love coached me. "Feel the character Frankie. Who is she? Is she happy or sad? Does she have worries? What does Frankie wonder about? Long for? Stand as Frankie would and speak loud enough for your audience to hear. You've been selected to audition...so be confident."

Miss Love was a smart and sensitive woman and made good suggestions. As we were leaving, "Good luck, Merilee," she wished me.

VALLEYS AND MOUNTAINS

As I reached home, I realized that, for more preparation, I'd need a tape recorder. I would act into the recorder and tape it. Then I would re-play it over and over again. This repetition would help me learn the lines.

I told this to Mom. "I'll ask your dad." she said.

Dad said no. He could not afford to pay for it.

Mom then mentioned this to Irving. In two days, Irving came by and handed me a good sized package. I unwrapped the big brown box to find the Wollensack tape recorder. I was so happy I threw my arms around Irving and kissed him on his check. I recorded the lines and I played them over and over again.

On the day of the audition I took the D train down to the 42nd Street stop and walked uptown to 46 Street, turning left. I found the school and the assigned schoolroom. My turn came and I performed the monologue.

> *"I told Bernice I was leavin' this town for good...and she didn't believe me. I kept on tellin' and tellin' her and tellin' her...Sometimes I think that woman's the biggest fool that ever drew breath..."*

Three teachers were present—two women and a man.

Mr. Jenkins, tall, thin with straight graying hair, was first to speak. "You have good stage energy"–a favorable comment, I knew. The other two teachers agreed, adding more comments. "You can leave now and you'll hear from the school," they told me.

I went home and every day went to the mailbox hoping I'd find something from The High School of Performing Arts. This was tedious, but I was very anxious and eager. One day it came and read,

> *"Dear Miss Sisapel, The High School of Performing Arts is pleased to inform you that you've been accepted into the drama department. On*

September 18, report to room 232 where we will set up your home room, and program your subjects."

I was thrilled and, telling Mom, I nearly flew through the roof of our apartment building. Mom was very happy for me.

That fall, I entered PA and met several students, many of whom spoke with this cultured diction. They sounded affected to me.

I shared this with a fellow student. "Several have probably come from professional families, which means they either mimic their parents' cultured diction, or have studied voice and diction," came the reply.

My mornings included drama, voice and diction and dance. Academics were scheduled for the afternoons.

In my very first semester I had a drama project with a student named Janet Margolin, who later went on to become a very good film actress.

Teachers, again, noted that my stage energy was very high and I received good ratings.

The second semester, in May, for my new project I performed a scene from the play, "My Sister Eileen." Teachers noted that my stage energy level had dropped significantly. They said I'd have to transfer to my local high school, Evander Child's, in The Bronx.

Broken-hearted, I took the train home. When I reached home, I just sat in our living room on our green club chair, very still. I did, however, share this with Mom, who consoled me and helped me apply to Evander.

At Evander that September, my marks had diminished. I didn't know why.

Getting through the semesters was tough. I was able to get a job that summer as a counselor in a local day camp. Here I found myself leaving the eight and nine year old kids who I was in charge of. frequently to go to the bathroom to urinate. Also, I was thirsty, hungry, losing weight, and tired.

One Saturday Mom and I went to a matinee where we saw *Marriage Go Round* starring Claudette Colbert. During intermission Mom and I went to the lavatory. Women patrons were standing on the line, washing their hands. I fainted. The matron helped revive me, likely, I later figured, with smelling salts, and Mom helped me stand up. We returned to our seats and saw the end of the play.

On the train coming home Mom said to me "I'm going to make an appointment for you to consult a diagnostician." She worked her magic, and that's what she did. We took a bus to this doctor's office. In his white lab coat, tall, thin with ruddy complexion, sparse gray hair and wire-rimmed eyeglasses, this doc appeared about 50 years old.

"Your urine sugar is very high and for that, I'll need further tests. You need to be admitted to Montefiore Hospital, across the street from your apartment building."

After admission and tests, in this hospital room with no pictures on the walls, just a tall plant in the corner–I was sitting on the bed. The resident doctor entered and sat next to me. Softly he said "Merilee, I have something serious to tell you."

"What is it doc? I have relatives with diabetes and I've been thirsty, hungry, eating more, tired and losing weight. And I've had the recent stress of my parents' separation. Also, I'm nearly sixteen years old and, like many adolescents, a flood of hormones is likely racing around in my system. Could this have produced diabetes?"

"Yes, you have diabetes," he answered. "However it is treated with diet, exercise and insulin and Dr. Troppauer, our intern, will guide you on all of this."

Dr. Troppauer came to my room and taught me how to use an orange and a syringe filled with some liquid and dart the syringe into the orange and plunge in the liquid. "This is like injecting insulin into your leg or tush," he told me. I quickly fell in love with this gentle soft-spoken man. As I was checking out of the hospital, I learned that Dr. T was engaged to be married. My dreams faded just as quickly as they'd arrived.

When I was released, at the office of the local family practitioner, Dr. Siegal gave me pamphlets on diet, exercise and insulin. Thus began my diabetes education. Returning home, Mom tried to help as best she could.

I entered Evander, and with tutors in geometry and chemistry that Mom arranged, and did very well. Friends were accepted at Hunter College where, to be admitted, students needed a very good average.

Sis had chosen to become a secretary and decided to work in Manhattan, where she'd gotten herself a job.

With my sagging Performing Arts baggage, I was concerned that my average might not be high enough. Dad provided a small living sum for Mom, Sis and me. I was pretty sure that paying a college tuition would be out of the question.

I got a job as a counselor at Camp NYDA, the camp for diabetic kids in Burlingham, NY, met terrific friends and attended the talk by invited guest Billy Talbert, the tennis star. His talk showed these campers with diabetes that, despite his insulin-dependent condition, he could be, and was, a champ.

And I met Thelma Waylerr, the camp dietician. She was terrific. She arranged campers' food plans and often counseled me privately. From some counselors I learned that because of campers restricted diets, many felt deprived and even sneaked off nights to the pantry and stole peanut butter, which they ate. It was more than likely that these *escapades* raised their blood sugars.

At NYDA, I also met Irv Wayler, Thelma's husband. Irv was a vocational counselor at New York State Division of Vocational

Rehabilitation. He worked in downtown New York. On my return home, I related this to Mom, who called him.

Mom phoned and told Irv: "Merilee's grades, we think, are unlikely to get into Hunter College and under my financial circumstances, we would not have money for a pay tuition.

"We'd like to get a scholarship for Merilee, and we'd appreciate it if you could help us arrange this."

Irv Wayler did his thing and got me an interview with some DVR rep. In the DVR Manhattan office, this lady gave me lots of academic tests on which I scored highly. This qualified me for a scholarship, and I was awarded a 4-year scholarship and chose to enroll in New York University on the Bronx campus, and enrolled.

I must have been trying too hard to overcome my rejections: from Dad, by whom, I felt abandoned; by Performing Arts; and by Mom, concerned with her own loss of husband. The 17 credits I took overloaded me. I worked very hard at my program, but couldn't do as well as I needed.

Anxious about me, Mom, tried to check on most of my urine sugars, and this gave me extra concern about my diabetes.

One lunchtime in the October sun, sitting out on the lawn with the students. All was nice. The students were having a good time talking and laughing, and sharing the bags of potato chips, peanuts, popcorn, Cracker Jacks. and sodas, they invited me to share. Sugared sodas, for me, were now *verboten*, and the other treats surely raised my blood sugars. This worked against my diabetes; nevertheless…

My energy had dropped, as did my marks. I was called to the office of the Dean of Scholarships, Dr, Janet Kennedy. Sitting behind her big mahogany desk, this husky woman, graying hair in a knot swept up to the top of her head, in her deep voice said, "I'm sorry, Merilee, but your grades are insufficient. We must rescind your scholarship."

So, again, heart torn apart, I returned home and told Mom.

Now I had to get a job.

Ever concerned about my diabetes, every time Mom knew that I peed, she kept checking my urine sugar tests. I felt self-conscious and different.

MONTEFIORE HOSPITAL

Good at numbers, Mom worked across the street from our home in Montefiore Hospital's Accounting Department, She was helpful and got me an interview with the head of the Home Care Department

Accepted, I became the department's receptionist. What a joy! I learned to operate a monitor board, and sat at the desk, and answered calls from patients and family members calling in to request medicines, and arrange visits with their social workers, doctors and recreation and occupational therapists. I had to transfer all these messages, and did very well, communicating with the staff and these patients, many of whom I really grew fond of.

One of the Home Care physicians, Dr. Robert Lowy, realized how I enjoyed this camaraderie. This very nice man, after checking my supervisors to see that the monitor board would be covered, invited me to accompany him on a home visit.

We visited patient Anna McCall. Dr. Lowy drove us in his car to the west Bronx address. We walked into this darkly lit building and took the elevator up to the fourth floor. Someone opened the apartment door and I met this elderly gray-haired, eye-glassed lady, sitting in her wheelchair, and gave her a great big hello. She did the same and when she learned it was me, the Home Care person with whom she'd spoken on the phone.

"Oh, Miss Merilee," Anna said, you're beautiful! I'm so glad to meet you in person." Her ear to ear smile revealed great happiness. We had a lovely time chatting. I felt accepted and valued.

I stepped away so Dr. Lowy could perform his physical exam and then we left.

About a year and a half on that job I decided I wanted to make more money. With the steno and typing I took in high school, I believed I could be a secretary, applied and got a position in the Hospital's Lydia Hall's Nursing Department.

A terrific endocrinologist Dr. Eugene Brody became my boss. Here, I'd take dictation and type the patient notes. I was fond of Dr. Brody as he was of me.

Dr. Brody later also became my endocrinologist. He saved my life one morning when Mom phoned him.

AT HOME, INSULIN REACTION

"Dr. Brody," Mom said, her quivering voice full of nerves. "Please help Merilee. She's in bed and unconscious and cannot take any juice."

"I'll be right over," said Dr. Brody and hung up. He arrived in about 10 minutes, Mom, later told me. It was my good fortune that Mom reached him when he was working across the street at Montefiore, so he could cross the street and come right over.

From his medical satchel he took out glucagon and promptly injected me with this medicine which raises blood glucose. He waited about 15 minutes until I awoke.

"Feeling better?" he asked, to which I replied,

"Yes, and what happened?"

"You had an insulin reaction. Too much insulin, too much exercise or not enough food. You should be okay soon," Dr. Brody told me and Mom.

When Dr. Brody sensed I was better, he suggested, "In about 10 minutes, Mrs. Sisapel, give Meri a glass of juice and check that she's okay. Then she can get up."

THE BRASS RAIL WORLD'S FAIR OPERATION

After nearly two years, I told Dr. Brody. "I want to make a change and work, like my sister, in the business world."

Dr. Brody said, "Hold on. I've got friends in the business world, and I'll call them."

A short while later, Dr. Brody gave me the number of a *Jay Emmett*. "Call him and say I referred you and that you want a job," Dr. Brody suggested.

THE PARTY

In between all this, Mom, (I think, hoping that I'd meet a nice doctor who would take care of me and my diabetes,) suggested that I make a party and invite a lot of doctors and friends from Montefiore. In addition to regular party foods–snacks, nuts and candies–Mom created a beautiful watermelon boat filled with cut up watermelon, honeydew, oranges and grapes. which, to this day, my friend, Aranka, remembers.

The party I arranged in our home was attended by lots of the interns, physical therapists and social workers. They arrived, greeted me, ate and danced to my phonograph records...and left.

I had met Aranka in Montefiore's dining room. Alone, eating my lunch, to my left I heard this lady speaking in Spanish. With my high school Spanish, I joined in.

"Hola, que tal?" I asked, meaning hello, *how are things?*.

"Habla Espanol?" this lady replied.

Then, I explained it was my high school Spanish and that I was really American.

"I'm from Chile," Aranka told me, and our conversation continued, almost never stopping.

After a while, we became good friends and room-mates.

Several months later, Aranka and I enjoyed a cruise together, venturing to Puerto Rico, Bermuda and St. Thomas. In San Juan, Aranka met Jose, from Puerto Rico, about 10 years older than she. They began a steamy love affair. In Bermuda, I befriended Ted. On his motorcycle, Ted drove me, sightseeing, all around the island.

Mom engaged a lawyer. Using her smarts and detective skills, she related her saga exposing Dad's attempt to get a Mexican Divorce.

A few weeks later, in the letter to Mom, this attorney congratulated her, showing that she, the "separated wife, rearing two children," was entitled to a substantial portion of Dad's retirement pension.

"This," mom told me, "enabled me to live independently."

SIS IN MANHATTAN

In a while, Sis had moved to a Manhattan apartment that she shared with friends Harriet and Ellie. Like my sister, I needed to get away from Mom and be on my own. Sis realized my problem and invited me to stay awhile in her West 34 Street apartment.

It felt good being away and taking care of myself. Believing that Mom was overly concerned with the results of my urine sugar tests, at that point I decided I'd not speak to Mom for six months, unless she needed me. This confused and hurt Mom deeply and left me plagued with guilt.

MY LEAVING HOME

After living with Sis and her roommates for a few weeks, I decided to definitely move out and searched for, and found, an apartment.

I was all packed and ready to leave our Bronx apartment, when the moving van arrived. I sat in the truck's passenger seat. Turning back towards Mom, I could see her standing on the stoop of our building, beating her chest and crying "Love's labor lost." I waved goodbye. This truck headed toward the apartment I'd rented on East 15 Street.

AD AND MERRILY GALE

From the apartment, I ran an ad for a roommate in the New York Times.

I was living there about a week when the phone rang. "What's your name?" I asked, into the phone, speaking to the young woman who answered my ad.

"Merrilly Haken," the sweet voice responded, to which I nearly fell off the bed laughing. I explained that, seeking a roommate for my Manhattan apartment, I ran the ad in the NY Times. It read: "Gal interested in theater, sports, people seeks same in room mate." "And my name was Merilee, too," I told her. Together we guffawed.

"I'm living at home with my folks in Wantagh and thinking of making the big move to the City," Merrily told me. We chatted and scheduled a date for this caller to come and view my apartment.

That Tuesday, I opened the door and this tall slim blonde well-spoken young woman entered. She looked at my apartment, noting "I've done the same Picasso Paint By Numbers paintings that hang on your walls," this Merrily shared.

Sitting at my dining table, conversing over coffee, Merrily told me that she wasn't yet sure about the apartment. "However, since we share interests, we can be friends and do things together. Good with you?" she asked.

"Sure is," I replied, and asked, "Where'd your parents get your name?

Terry and The Pirates Comic Strip,'" this Merrily told me.

I replied, "I'm told that this comic strip-Merrily was the pig-tailed and freckled-faced character that my sister, Elaine, loved. My parents needed an 'm' name because I was named after my grandmother Malia."

Merrily was ready to leave and we both agreed to keep in touch.

Approaching my apartment's door, I shared, "My middle name is Dale, and that June, as a newborn, being checked out of the Lenox Hill Hospital, the head nurse told my mother that they had just checked out another newborn, by the name of Merrily Gale or something. Growing up, my mother, time after time, introducing me, I heard this story over and over, and it stuck.

Mom would say, "This is our daughter, Merilee Dale…"

It was April and though really 22 years old, and, curious, I aged myself, "I'm 23, by the way, and how old are you?"

"I'm 22. I'll be 23 in June." My jaw dropped, eyes opening wide.

"And I was born at Lenox Hill Hospital," she told me.

"You were the baby!" I exclaimed," my finger pointing to Merrily. We both laughed so hard that I am sure it could have been heard across Long Island and beyond. We did become roommates a while later. The phone would ring and the caller, asking for "Merrily," would get our "Which one–Merrily Gale or Merrily Dale?"

BRASS RAIL WORLD'S FAIR

Shortly thereafter I got in touch with Dr. Brody's friend Jay Emmett who put me in touch with a man named Guy Beaudine. Mr. Beaudine was the licensing manager of the Brass Rail Restaurant's World's Fair operation.

Three

1965

I went downtown to meet with Mr. Beaudine in the Brass Rail Restaurant on Broadway and 49 Street. The upstairs was dark, not well lit. In the dingy office, the meeting went well and I was hired. It was great to meet all the licensees, some of whom took me to lunch. I did good work for Mr. Beaudine and felt satisfied.

Working for Mr. Beaudine for a little over a year, I'd learned he used to drive down to New York from his Connecticut home.

The Fair opened and our licensing operation was moved to Flushing Meadows, to a warehouse where the Fair merchandise to be unpacked, was stored, then moved to the Fairgrounds, and sold.

I met lots of vendors and lunched in Flushing.

Fair merchandise was housed and unloaded here and workers' checks were delivered to this location. One day, the truck was late–very late–and the workers–black, white and Hispanic men–were getting angry.

I hid my fear, and facing this large crowd, put my acting skills to work. Brave yet sensitive face applied, I walked into the main room and told these workers, "Please be patient. We've been in touch with the payroll department, and they assured us that your checks will arrive shortly." Fortunately, the checks did arrive, and content, the workers went home.

I met many licensees, many of whom would take me out to lunch On one occasion I met licensee Norm Cohn from Waterloo, Iowa. Norm was, what I considered attractive: tall, slim with dark curly hair, and well-spoken. Late one afternoon, he invited me to go, with him, to dinner, including wine, and the theater.

After the show, he had a cab drive us to the Forest Hills Inn and checked us in. Next thing I remember was that, in the morning, I found a red stain on my side of the bedsheet and realized that here I had lost my virginity. Too much wine, I guessed. Or the wine and my diabetes didn't go well together.

Norm and I avoided this topic of conversation. We took a cab into the City. He dropped me off at 59 Street and Fifth Avenue–across from the Bronx Zoo–and we said goodbye.

That's how it goes, I told myself. I didn't have a crush on Norm. I didn't have time to consider the meaning of this or my feelings about myself.

One day, arriving in the office, word came that Mr. Beaudine had been killed in a car accident. I felt bad, because he was a nice man. There was also the realization at the back of my mind that I needed a new job.

By this time, Merrily Gale moved into a relationship with a man named Ernst, and left my apartment to live in New Jersey. I, too, had moved from 15th Street and gotten a studio apartment on West 86 Street.

Here, my dad visited me and, with his police training and awareness of drugs on the upper west side, seeing my fire escape window, he suggested that I get a gate for this window. I did, grateful for his awareness, care and suggestion.

Also, around this time, in Greenwich Village, from traders at the street fair I'd attended, I purchased a second hand piano. A truck I'd hired moved the piano up to this apartment. And the $20 shipping price was the same as the price I paid for the piano.

As a kid, Dad used to enjoy hearing me play and sing, This day, "Would you like me to play and sing a song or two?" I asked, and he said yes. I was happy to have Dad as my audience, and so I sang and played.

LEGAL SECRETARY

I got a job with Mr. Beaudine's attorney Fred Pagnani. His office was in Manhattan, and I became a legal secretary and took my case notes and went downtown to courts. Some days, he wanted me to take the NY Central Railroad up to his home in Rye, New York. At Rye, the cab I hailed took me to his address.

It was a large beautiful colonial style house and his attractive blonde wife Ginny welcomed me in. I met Mr. P in the well-appointed den, sat in a large club chair and took dictation. After it was over, I enjoyed their chicken salad sandwich and coffee, then the ride in another cab to the station for the return railroad trip.

A short while later I got word that Mr. Pagnani had legal problems and he was going to have to let me go. However he put me in touch with the people from The Shubert Organization.

THE SHUBERT ORGANIZATION

The Shubert Organization–I was thrilled! This was closer to my dream of acting–hopefully on Broadway. The Shuberts owned most of the Broadway theaters.

I came to work for Abe Baranoff, a short feisty well-dressed man who, secretly, once in a while, snuck a puff of one of his cigars. Always with a cheery expression and something jovial to say, Mr. Baranoff was in charge staffing the box offices in New York and all the out of town Shubert Theatres. I was Mr. Baranoff's administrative assistant.

Working at the Shubert's, all this time, I'd see all the shows coming into Broadway. Press agents and company managers contacted me saying, for their new show–straight play or musical–they were "papering the house" on such and such night and asked, "Would you please help fill it?"

I'd call all my friends and, offering the free tickets, I'd tell them to go to the box office, on a particular evening, and say "Abe Baranoff sent me. They'd get in and would see the show–for free.

My love of acting persisted. On my own time, I took classes in the City, with a recommended teacher Warren Robertson. In his West 48 Street loft studio, I learned exercises to relax and feel free to release emotions, such as anger and love. This meant, onstage, I had to shake my shoulders and body, stamp my feet and vocally grunt to release whatever pent up feelings were inside me. I also learned to do improvisations and scenes.

Frequently alone after class, I went across the street to the Greek diner and bought a bag of zeppoles. Riding home on the 8th Avenue bus, trying to keep the powdered sugar from getting on my clothes and the floor, privately, I gobbled them down.

Was this the cause of blood sugar swings? Emotions? I didn't think of this and didn't know. I just sought the comfort of the zeppoles.

Years later, my eating disorder was diagnosed. After many sessions, but no success, with Overeaters Anonymous, I was referred to recommended psychiatrist Dr. Willard Kahn. After work, I'd come to his Madison Avenue office with the bag of cookies I'd picked up. Prior to our session, in the waiting room, I tackled these.

With his horn rimmed tortoise shell glasses and herringbone sports jacket and slacks, he sat in his recliner, me in the other. Questions like: "Anything you'd like to tell me?" made me open up very little. But mostly, he would let me sit and, if and when I wanted, talk. I got very little from this.

After two years and no progress, Dr. Kahn suggested I needed more intense psychotherapy. I could not afford his fee twice a week. So he made a referral to the Columbia Psychoanalytic Clinic.

From the Overeaters Anonymous meetings, I learned here that every action has a reaction. Everything I put into my mouth adds calories and weight and affects my blood sugar.

Happily, at the Columbia Psychoanalytic Clinic, I was accepted and began the two-year program as the patient of Dr. Anne E Bernstein.

With Dr. Bernstein's therapy, I learned how my eating binges were often caused by blood sugars–high or low–and also, emotions. Emotions anger and love were part of the human condition and were allowed. Blood sugars in control, I had no need to binge-eat. And, emotions accepted and released, I'd no longer have to stuff them down, by eating forbidden foods.

I worked on many ways to release my pent up emotions with Dr. Bernstein. One was to paint my feelings in pastels on a pad on my apartment floor.

One picture I created was on a red background. The stick figure I drew lay on the floor. The other stick figure representing me, was standing, with a scythe in my hand. It showed that I'd done the deed of the anger in my heart. I framed it and gave it to Dr. Bernstein. She hung it on the wall of her new office.

Dr. Bernstein also told me of the psychiatrist who discovered the connection between emotions and overeating. I read up on Dr Bruch and wrote an article explaining this, which was later published in the New York Daily News.

HOME GLUCOSE MONITORING

It was 1970 and home glucose monitoring was coming into vogue. This meant people with diabetes could now test their own blood sugars on glucose meters, and treat themselves, at home–or wherever they traveled.

We could carry our meters with us, as I did. Dr. Bernstein's husband Richard, already an engineer, now studying to be a doctor, like me, grew up with juvenile-onset diabetes. He learned all about diabetes and shared the nuances with his wife. So, Dr. Anne was well-versed on this disease and shared her knowledge with me. She also suggested that I join a group teaching home glucose monitoring. I did and it changed my life!

I'd learned that for Dr. B, her work with me was part of her training. Nearing the end of my two year program, she invited me to be the guest speaker at her session. This would show her colleagues and instructors her progress with me–particularly that I could be in touch with my emotions. "Certainly I'll take part," I agreed.

The event was scheduled to take place at the Columbia Psychoanalytic Clinic in a small auditorium. The attendees sat on benches. I entered and saw Dr. B in her chair, and she beckoned me to join her. We both faced the audience of about 20 men and women student-psychiatrists, like she, studying for their graduation from training.

Facing this group, I was seated with Dr. B. She made a brief introduction.

"This is Merilee Sisapel and I've been working to help Merilee accept and release her emotions and recover from her eating disorder.

"So, welcome, Merilee."

"Thanks, Dr. Bernstein," I replied. I'm pleased to be here and happy to share my experiences with your group."

So began this meeting at which I shared, for example, an anecdote of my neighbor-friends enjoying life with their mom and rotund dad.

"After dinner, I'd go next door to my friends' apartment. The sisters' bedroom is where we'd get together and play games or talk. On the way, we'd pass the living room, where I saw their dad, Al, eating his chocolate covered bon bons and laughing at the tv game shows. Mom Ester was in the kitchen talking on the telephone and sewing something on her sewing machine.

The mom and pop would laugh and sometimes yell at each other. However, at 7:30 every morning, together they'd travel downtown to work in their belt factory and come home together, and with their kids, my friends, they'd eat their dinners.

I told the group, "Now my dad is out of our house and right next door is this happy family, and I no longer have this family-laughing, scolding and love."

Reminiscing, I began to cry a bit.

I shared a few other memories, too, evoking more tears. Then it was all over.

Dr. Bernstein and the group thanked me for attending, and I left.

In an office session with Dr. Bernstein, she had explained that after this two-year program, if I ever needed her I could reach her in her office by phone or private visit.

Knowing I was a publicist, I received a call one evening and she told me her daughter was getting married. .

"I want to ask a favor. Do you think you could put a notice of the upcoming marriage on the New York Times Weddings page? she asked.

I told her I'd need particulars and I'd get it into format and forward it. Then we'd see.

So she sent the info to me. I posted it and in about two weeks it appeared.

I was pleased I could do this for her.

THE HAMPTONS AND MEETING HERB

Years were moving on and friends were getting married. Many of them had met husbands at The Hamptons, the place, I'd learned, where people in their 20's and 30's went to hunt for spouses.

I bought a house-share in East Hampton. Here, share-members shopped, cleaned, cooked and enjoyed mate-hunting at the beach.

One day, in my red and green floral print bathing suit, walking the beach, I heard, "Hey, she looks like a tennis player," the male voice, told his friend. It was coming from my right side, below, perhaps in a sand chair.

I turned, batted my eyelashes and coyly replied, "Who me?"

"Yes, you play tennis?" the male voice continued.

"Yes," I replied. "You, too?"

MERILEE KAUFMAN

I turned and saw this eye-glassed man, baseball cap shading his head, resting comfortably in a sand chair.

"Yes, and I'm Herb Kaufman. What's your name?"

"I'm Merilee Sisapel."

Herb told me he was an art teacher in the New York City school system.

"I'm a publicist and work for a small publicity firm in the City. I'm beginning my "time-share" week in a house in East Hampton.

We chatted, played some frisbee, volleyball, catch and dipped in the ocean, too. Herb took my phone number and beach house address.

We got to know each other. At Martell's, the local bar and hangout, Van Morrison's MOONDANCE set us happily dancing musical moves. And we drank some: for me, a glass of wine and for Herb, a beer. We also had fun doing lindy's, cha-chas and fox-trots. Over several restaurant dinners, we got to know each other.

Herb took me to a fine restaurant called John Duck, Jr.s. He ordered the duck for him, and I chose the same. My portion consumed, Herb asked, "How was it?"

"Very good," I said. "Could I please have another order?"

Herb ordered, and I downed, the whole second order. "I was hungry," I explained. Both of us satisfied and happy, we left.

I thought to myself, here I was with a guy who was accommodating my every desire!

EGYPTIAN DATE

I was at *The Hamptons*, on vacation and there for fun and hubby-hunting. No strings–or rings yet. I was still free.

One day, wandering to the shore, a well-built young man came up beside me and said, "Hello, my name is Jamil. May I know your name?"

His complexion was dark–middle-eastern looking–and like his black hair, and he had a mustache and thin beard. His voice was deep. In addition to the print bathing suit on his frame, he wore a smile.

Hmmmm, I thought–an *Omar Sharif* look-alike.

"I'm Merilee."

"You like to swim,?" he asked.

"Yes, but not in the ocean. I enjoy swimming in pools."

"Oh," Jamil continued. "I have a job at the Maidstone Arms. If you like, you could be my guest in their pool. It's on the rooftop. I don't have a car, so you'll have to get yourself there"

"Thank you. Tell me a bit about yourself," I inquired. "Where are you from?"

"Well, I come from Egypt" said Jamil. "After the season, I work in the City."

"What do you do there?"

"I work at a diner."

I dipped my toes in the gently bubbling water, then said, "Let me answer you tomorrow. What date and time were you thinking of?

"As soon as you'd like."

"Okay. I can tell you tomorrow, about this time. Good for you?

"Yes, it is."

I left and walked back, actually to Herb.

"Who were you talking to?," Herb asked.

"Some guy I met," I replied. "And Herb, would you drive me to the Maidstone Arms tomorrow evening? This guy invited me to use their pool, so I'll be able to use the pool and get some lap-swimming in."

"Okay." Then he thought for a moment, and continued, "Sure."

I had secured my lift.

Now I'd have to arrange that I don't get raped by Jamil. I'd think about it. .

I know, I thought, I'll tell him that, at the appropriate time that I have a lift waiting.

At about 4pm, I met Jamil on the beach and told him that yes, I'd be happy to take advantage of his invitation.

"Be at the Maidstone rooftop pool at about 10 pm. At this late hour, we'll have the pool to ourselves, and I'll be there."

At the appropriate time, I was there, and Herb agreed to call for me at about 11:30.

I dressed in my bathing suit and did not bring my diaphragm. I was determined I was not going to have sex with Jamil.

Plush leather chairs, mirrors on the ceiling and velvet couches in the lobby, I took the elevator to the rooftop.

""Hello," said Jamil, as I got off the elevator. He took my hand and led me across to the pool. It was spacious and had a diving board. Pointing, on the right to the set of white plastic chairs, Jamil said, "You can leave your bags over there on the chair and jump into the pool. The water temperature is about 82."

Sounded good to me. "But," I asked, "What will you do while I swim?"

"I'll dive in and swim some, too. You can come out when you're ready and dry off. You'll have to shower elsewhere."

The whole pool to ourselves–no interference. Wonderful! So I jumped into the chlorinated pool and began doing my laps. The water immersion felt wonderful. On every turn, I looked and found Jamil also doing some laps. Then he got out of the pool and dried off with his towel, his eyes following me. My eyes followed him and I could admire his lean, well- muscled physique. Standing, he appeared taller than Herb.

At about 11:10, my waterproof Timex watch told me to get out and dry off. That's what I did.

"You swam well. How did you enjoy it?" asked Jamil.

"Very much," I replied, "and now I've got to go home. Can you please take me downstairs, so I can meet my driver."

"Surely," said Jamil. "But I'm happy to do this again for you. Would you like to?" he asked.

"Perhaps. I'll meet you on the beach if and when it's good for me. Okay with you?" I asked.

"Yes, okay. And would you like to stop for a coffee now," he asked.

Okay, I thought, here comes his pitch: *coffee, the room he could borrow, and more.*

"No, thanks. I've got to meet my ride. But thanks again for this treat," I said, then took the elevator to the lobby, exited, and met Herb.

HERB'S REACTION

"Hi, Mer." said Herb as I opened the car door and got in. "How was your swim?"

"Terrific, Herb, and so glad you could get here to pick me up."

Herb kept looking around at the hotel entrance and exit, I expect, to see if he could spot my date.

No one in sight, we headed back.

"Will you do this again?" Herb asked.

"Don't know now. I'll think about it. But I really don't want to trouble you. Guess I can call a cab."

"No, don't do that. It's really no trouble and I'll be happy to do it. That exercise is good for you," said my selfless Herb.

I never repeated this Jamil-date. Yet Herb kept asking, about every month, and every year after that–"Have you seen that man again–or heard from him?"

"No," I replied. And probably will never again."

After a week or so of more beaching, getting acquainted and Herb giving me tours of The Hamptons, Herb suggested he'd make squab for dinner for us in the home he shared there with friend Gene.

After some time at the beach, shopping for food and refrigerating purchases, "Let's take a shower together," Herb suggested. With trepidation, naked, soap-bathed washcloths in hand, we carefully climbed into the shower. I washed Herb's arms, back and legs and gave him the washcloth for his penis. Herb's hands and washcloth washed my arms, legs and back, gently reaching my private parts.

"Later..." I suggested, and so we waited.

MADE HERB AWARE OF MY DIABETES

I found Herb to be gentle, soft-spoken, humble, sweet, giving and quite brilliant–with a terrific sense of humor. He knew all the old films, movie stars. He'd studied and played the mandolin, taught himself guitar and was in his high school orchestra. He was familiar with all the singers and musicians–both popular and classical–of the 30's and 40's.

His mom had been in The Mandolin Orchestra and Herb got his mandolin training from her. I was the extrovert here, my voice and diction training from Performing Arts helped. And I still loved acting.

My week completed, city-bound regulars with cars packed, share-owner--luggage filling the trunk and laps, we headed home. Just inside my apartment door, I raced to my ringing phone.

"Hello, who is this?" I asked.

The gentle voice on the other end replied, "It's Herb. Just wanted to know if you arrived safely."

I was so happy that someone cared.

"I'm here safely, dear Herb, and I'm so glad you cared and called," I told this sweet and kind pursuer.

DIABETES

I had made Herb aware of my insulin-dependent diabetes, at times, requiring that I take sugar or orange juice to raise my blood sugar to safe levels. Low blood sugars were often a side-effect of the exercise.

After returning to the City, I had invited Herb to stay at my apartment on West 86 Street weekend mornings. We'd play tennis in nearby Central Park, often going for a snack or breakfast later.

One day, at the corner diner: "What will you have?" the Greek waiter asked.

"I'd like *orangutang* juice," I replied.

"We don't have that on the menu. So what else can I get you?"

Herb ordered his juice, then tried to help solve the verbal puzzle.

"What's that, Mer?" After several times, and having learned to sense and treat my low blood sugars, Herb asked me, "You mean orange juice?" A smile beamed across my face and I nodded affirmatively, tapped his hand then blew him a kiss. Herb requested the orange juice.

After dinner, one evening driving down Second Avenue to the Public Theater for a show, I said, "Herb, please pull the car over and stop at a grocery store or bodega. I need a can of whipped cream."

Accommodatingly, Herb double-parked the car, got out and went into the bodega, coming out with a can of Reddi Whip whipped cream. I removed the red lid-cap and pressed the nozzle, spray after spray, the white sugar-filled foamy cream emptied into my mouth, sliding down my gullet. Feeling better, we proceeded to the show.

So began our formal courtship. Herb was now 35 years old and I, 28. After the summer, Herb returned to his position in the NYC school system and I to my publicity position.

Herb was still living in his mom's home in Brooklyn, and wanting to get a place of his own. I encouraged and supported this move to the apartment he'd found on Ocean Parkway. Together we shopped for his dining room set and couch and a bed. Pictures on the wall, too.

Weekends, Herb would drive into New York to stay at my apartment, getting up early to move his white Ford Valiant to meet parking regulations.

Herb, strong, brilliant, passionate and humble, wrote this poem on a little piece of note paper and one day handed it to me.

Herb's WHO IS MERILEE
To Mer, August 1970

In the pounding, sounding
rhythm, In the swirling
blurring of faces, like
from a speeding carousel.
In the rising, blaring volume,
I look for you.

In the raucous grins of teeth, In the
shaking and the snaking.
In the sweet stench
of sweat and scotch
and smoke, I gaze above
the haze and look for you.

Amid the endless music,
the searching eyes,
the sad laughter
and the clutching,
groping, hoping bodies --
attracting, repelling, attracting,
lingering, like mixed up
magnets, I look for
your face.

In the sober chilling warmth
of the sometime sun,
in the silence of the sands,
the suffering sea
repeats its gloomy story.

Your love
is a fragile footprint, to be
erased by wind or wave,

by will or whim.

You are beside me,
breathing, speaking, touching–
all life, all love, all truth.
You are here,
but still I must ask,
"Who are you?"

You are you–
goodness and warmth,
softness and heart–all charm.
But still I ask,
"Who are you?

Can you be mine?
Glorious form–wonder and wit
and wisdom.
Child and sage, and
I must ask, "Who are you?"

Here are two humorous gems by Herb:

Picking your toes is far
superior to picking
your nose.

My frontal lobotomy
took a lot out 'o me.

A MASQUERADE PARTY

It was October 31. Merrily Gale and Ernst planned a Halloween party and invited me and Herb. It would be at Merrily and Ernst's new home in New Jersey.

Herb and I decided to dress up as Pierrot and Pierrette, the orphan characters from the 1924 film. Herb dressed in black slacks, a white shirt and black shoes, belt and beret. I applied lipstick to my darling's lips and lipstick smudges to rouge his cheeks. My costume was similar: white slacks and white flowing clown-like jacket with big black puff buttons, also a black beret, and the same make-up.

Our gas tank was full and with directions Merrily had given me, we got in our car and headed west. Nearly there I realized I needed a restroom. So we stopped at a gas station. I got out. and in my outfit, asked the attendant. "Can I use your ladies room, please?"

A startled look appeared on the young attendant's face. Seeing my outfit, his eyes opened in wide surprise. "We're dressed for a Halloween party," I explained. He directed me toward the key hanging from a lanyard outside the bathroom door. I thanked him, relieved myself and we moved forward.

Five

MY SISTER, ELAINE

Sis, six years my senior, pug-nosed, brown hair and marble-size eyes had big breasts. She was beautiful–a Joan Collins look-alike, Mom said. She wore make-up, jewelry, got her hair done at Larry Matthews beauty salon. And she dated, often coming home late. Mom's only discipline: chasing Sis around the kitchen table, trying to hit her with a hanger or yardstick.

Needing my mother's love, I tried to push the kitchen table into Sis–to halt her–so my Mom could reach her. Years later, my sister later told me that for decades she held this against me.

Sis had been a good singer. In her high school production of Gilbert and Sullivan's *HMS Pinafore*, Sis played the lead role: Buttercup.

She dated, and had a close relationship with Ron, a handsome lawyer from a Spanish family. He loved and wanted to marry my sister.

Dad had been a policeman. My sister met, and chose Larry, a Dad look-a-like–tall and also on The Force. They were engaged. After all the presents and good wishes, the two broke up.

FREDDIE

Sis had met Freddie, a stocky rugged looking man who, I thought, spoke like a thug. "I was born in Brooklyn and work at Riker's Island, guarding prisoners–a stressful operation," Freddie told us when we met.

"So stressful," he continued, "that I learned to smoke pot–to calm me down."

"I smoke some, too," my sister shared.

The two both enjoyed old films, art, history and antiques. This fit right in with Sis, as a side line, getting into the antiques business.

After working as a secretary for years, Sis finally pursued her yearning for and collecting jewelry, old paintings and lamps from little old ladies in Manhattan. A young antiques dealer was born.

Sis and Freddie married on December 5. Herb and I were invited to their celebration-lunch at Luchow's–a German restaurant in lower Manhattan. The couple also invited a pair of their friends. However, they had invited neither our mother nor father.

Freddie recently retired. Together, weekends in Manhattan, the two took part in selling at different street fairs. For this, they packed goods and display tables, and took cabs to get them to different locations. With her "Renaissance Antiques" business title, brains and outgoing personality, my sister became well-known and respected.

At her antiques business, Sis told me that British singer Cleo Laine perused her goods. Comedienne Joan Rivers also shopped at Sis' stall, Rivers being, Sis shared, really cheap.

At her love-vocation, Sis earned a good living. So good, in fact, that she often needed help, and would often invite me or Mom to host the table with her, be alert for thefts and help sell. For thanks, Sis gave me and Mom each a small trinket of antique jewelry.

ACTING AND THE SHUBERTS

While working for The Shuberts I met and was friendly with Shubert attorneys Schoenfeld and Jacobs. Both brilliant and light-hearted, balding eye-glassed attorney Gerry Schoenfeld often kidded, chasing me around his desk. His belly carried a slight middle-aged paunch.

Herb and I would attend many Off-Off Broadway and I'd found Ensemble Theatre, whose productions were excellent. I knew that I wanted to appear in one of their shows.

At the time, calls for auditions were usually advertised in trade newspapers. At the auditions, so many aspiring actors and actresses lined up! We would take numbers and wait for our turn till maybe 600 actors were called. I told Mr. Schoenfeld about my ambition and said I'd love to perform in one of the shows of Ensemble Studio Theater–but I couldn't stand to wait for 600 additions.

The Shuberts donated money to lots of theatrical ventures. In a few days, Mr. Schoenfeld told me to call Ensemble, say I was from The Shuberts and an audition would be arranged. I needed a monologue.

By this time, I was working as a secretary, then publicist, for a publicity firm named Bernie Ilson, Inc. Bernie's wife Carol had been in theater and directed some small shows. I told her of my wish and the Ensemble opportunity and she helped me.

We selected a comedic monologue from the film *Who Is Harry Kellerman and Why is He Saying Those Terrible Things About Me*. Carol coached me, I made the call, and got the audition date. With a photo and resume, make-up and hair in place and Herb at my side, I showed up.

After introductions, I ascended the small Off Off Broadway stage and performed my monologue, getting laughs from the theater audience staff in appropriate places.

At the end, I asked the stage manager, "What next?"

"Leave your resume and photo. When we have an appropriate part, we'll call you."

I was happy that I got the laughs and that they said they would call me.

I was also thrilled that I had Herb with me, because by this time I had begun to love him and realized that I wanted to spend the rest of my life with this man. And I knew that Herb loved me.

GREEN MOUNTAIN

NYDA's Thelma Wayler, in season, a nutrition educator at Long Island University, and I kept in touch and a few times, she and husband Irv dined with Herb and me. While working for Bernie, he told me that if I brought in a client to the firm, he'd give me a percentage of their fee.

After leaving NYDA, Thelma established a weight control community called GREEN MOUNTAIN AT FOX RUN. Providing basically an education in nutrition, exercise and behavioral control, it was a getaway place in Vermont where women from around the world could reside for a period of time and learn to become the women they wanted to be. All they had to do was lose the weight they wanted to. It started as a two month program, but participants could attend for an additional two weeks or more, as well.

I'd get my 15% fee of the participants monthly bill–a nice additional income for me. And, at Bernie's, the publicity I did on Green Mountain helped the community grow–especially the visit I arranged for NY Times Living Section reporter Judy Klemesrud. This drew women from around the world–wherever the NY Times was read.

Six

INTRODUCTIONS: ME TO ANNA, AND ME AND HERB TO MOM, AND US TO DAD AND BETTY

Back to me and love. I learned that what I was seeking was not the audience reaction. Rather it was love. Herb and I got on very well. He was quiet and I was outgoing. The years were moving on. By this time I knew that Herb was wonderful and wanted to marry me, and I loved and wanted to marry him.

First, I had to meet Herb's mom.

One sunny Sunday morning, I said to Herb, "It's time. Introduce me to your mother, please." So on a clear crisp March morning. we got into Herb's car and drove up the parkways to get to Herb's mom's house in Brooklyn. We climbed the stairs, opened the door and stepped inside.

My mom's three and a half room apartment was beautiful–everything neatly in place and in perfect order.Mom had beautiful taste and I could see the results of her school training in art and design. She managed very well on her limited budget. For example, she'd bought a piece of marble-design contact paper and placed it over a crack on our living room coffee table. Herb's mom's house was starkly different.

We were met by this little lady in her apron with shreds, gray hair pulled back and held in place with a barrette and bobby pins. She was missing several teeth. Yet, a big smile lit her face.

Herb introduced me, "Mom, this is Merilee, my girlfriend." Anna was so happy she put her arms around me and hugged tight. I was so grateful, I hugged right back. Unafraid, she was utterly loving. Then she offered us something to eat and whatever cracker I took, she offered more.

In her raggedy surroundings, this house was not beautiful nor elegant like my mom's apartment. Here, linoleum was broken and ripped. The plastic tablecloth was torn. as was her apron. But her love transformed it into a mansion.

I loved writing poetry and, while working in the City, I had applied to, was accepted, and had become a member of The Poetry Society of America. After meeting Anna, among poems I wrote was *Anna, My Mother-In-Law*.

ANNA, MY MOTHER-IN-LAW

A left-eye that squints,
Gray straight barrette-clipped hair.
White cotton socks in black slippers,
a decade old, meant for a man.
A nubby orlon sweater tucked into
zipper-broken plaid slacks
held together by a long piece of wool.
A big smile that spreads across her face
when her family comes to visit.
A woman who gave her wedding band
and gold jewelry to her daughter in-laws
to enjoy. Anna, my mother-in-law.

Weekly, she'd serve us a full-course dinner:
melon, soup with kneidlach,
chicken, a starch, a vegetable,
fruit and nuts for dessert.

For her failing eyes,
we'd clear places on the table
so she could set the meal down.

"What else can I get you," she'd ask, "to nosh.

This evening at our house she watches tv, feet on a hassock to reduce swelling.

After our day's work, the meal is simple. She chooses noodles and cheese. She cannot chew the salad. "No dessert, thanks," she says.

When I tell her she's given me so much and I can offer so little, she asks, "So when can I do it, again?"

Attendance at most of Anna's Friday night dinners included Herb's Uncle Irving and his girlfriend Anna Marie and Herb's brother Jerry and his girlfriend Renee'. This brought more love into Anna's life, and more into mine.

Herb's dad, I learned, had died several years before.

I knew I wanted to marry Herb and he finally asked me. I was thrilled and told my Mom and friends. I had developed asthma by then and got shot treatments from an allergist.

Now, I had to have Herb to meet both my mother and father

Mom was aging, and at times Herb and I would shop for her–or if she preferred, we'd take her to her neighborhood Key Food store. We'd also take her, occasionally, to her internist. Otherwise, despite our suggestion that she take cabs, for which we'd pay, she 'd take one or two buses.

Our mother Sylvia, had studied design, and had great style in fashion and furnishings.

Now in her early eighties, Mom lived in and managed the apartment in which she raised my sister and me. Attractive and smart, she was a great cook, attended functions of Hadassah and ORT, continued to shop for herself, have her hair done, she still dressed well and applied rouge onto her cheeks and lipstick. One time, from an ORT bazaar, she lugged home for me a framed print by Leroy Nieman. It hangs in our apartment to this day.

I wrote this poem prompted by Mom's visits to the beauty parlor:

SOPHISTICATED RED

So young, she thinks,–the manicurists –
and Korean –
in the salon where they paint her nails
Sophisticated Red.

Fingers of her right hand soak.
Left-right, left-right goes the emery board.
As the bassist bows strings, the manicurist files.
Young woman, intent in her art.

A worker sits at an adjacent table,
asks her associate for a piece of gum.
Another playfully snatches a packet of sugar
from the drawer. In their language
they share a story, giggling.
I could be their mother, she thinks.

Their youth–barretted curled hair,
skin unwrinkled, smooth as soap bubbles –
tells her age.
She sees herself a child of ten
with her mother in

Manny's Beauty Salon in The Bronx.
Thursday, her mother's day
for a wash, set and manicure: Windsor Rose.
After school, pigtailed,
in a gingham or plaid dress,
she wanders in to be close.

Her eyes fix on the beautician
winding her mother's strawberry blonde hair
into pin curls and metal rollers,
then setting her under the dryer.

Sapphire cigarette smoke,
the sulphuric smell of Toni Permanents
inundate the dark narrow shop.

Hands outstretched for the manicurists,
patrons–grown up women—
half their heads under humming dryers,
sit flipping pages of True Romance, McCall's.
Services completed, "beautified,"
their blue or blonde hair
sprayed stiff enough to halt a hurricane,
customers press coin tips
into their beauticians' pink smock pockets.

Sitting waiting patiently,
she knows her mother is
always there.

Today she is the age
her mother was then.

In the contest run by CW Post College on Long Island, this was published in the college's journal *Confrontation*, and it won the 2nd prize)

MEETING MY MOM

I brought Herb up to The Bronx one night to meet my mother. Mom had prepared dinner for me and Herb and Sis and Freddie. She wore an attractive fuchsia hostess robe. Strawberry blonde hair freshly coiffed, she looked lovely,

And Sis, with her heavy, theatrical-looking dark eye makeup and jewelry looked good, too, as did Freddie. And after a little glass of wine, we sat down to eat Mom's dinner of salad, half a grapefruit, delicious pot roast, potatoes, and vegetables. We all chatted and it worked out nicely.

One more introduction: Dad and his new companion, Betty.

MEETING DAD AND BETTY

Herb and I drove to Dad's home–the apartment in Sunnyside, Queens, that he shared with Betty. Under slacks, covering his prostheses for his below the knee amputation due to his diabetes, Dad opened the apartment door.

I introduced Dad to Herb. Dad's welcoming was very friendly. "I'm so glad to meet you," he told Herb. "Come right in...." We entered and Dad then introduced us to Betty.

Dad had told me that Betty was a widow and that she never had children. I could see that she was eager to meet and befriend me–and, I thought, even think of me as her missing child.

Betty's black hair was coiffed and with an apron over her house-dress, she wore white-gold bracelets studded with diamonds. Lipstick-smeared lips, when she smiled, showed how glad she was to meet us.

Betty spoke loudly, likely, I suspect due to her loss of hearing, and she was boastful of her brother Matthew, the lawyer, her sister Frieda, and her nephews, and the money she claimed they had.

While I helped bring the food dishes to the table, Herb sat on the sofa with Dad and chatted. Daily, Dad read the newspaper and he and Herb spoke about the world and politics. My quiet man revealed himself, speaking about his occupation, his art and music, hobbies and sports. We sat down to eat and enjoy Betty's good cooking, and all was fine.

On the way home, from Herb: "After what you'd mentioned about your parents separation and your father's threat, I was surprised to find your Dad so engaging and nice."

It was now up to us.

Seven

OUR WEDDING

Dad said he did not have money for a wedding ceremony. It was up to Mom. The wedding would be at Temple Young Israel on Avenue J in Brooklyn. Mom would pay for the reception, and we would choose a restaurant nearby.

I was reluctant to invite Dad because I knew the problems I'd encounter with Mom. Mom said, "I do not want that woman, Betty, at the dinner arranged for you that I'm paying for."

Dad needed Betty to come and be part of this.

It was quite clear! Mom would not have Betty at the restaurant.

You must realize, as Dad told me privately, that Betty often bragged about her wealth in stocks and bonds. And she claimed that she contributed most of the finances of this pair. If she's not invited, Betty will not give money as a wedding gift.

I then spoke with my psychiatrist, Dr. Bernstein about my reluctance to invite Dad and Betty. "You tell him that he's your only father, you're his child, and that it's vital to you to have him at *your* wedding."

Extremely nervous, I did finally relate to Dad what Dr. Bernstein had told me.

Having, for all my life, been a perfectionist, head to toe, top to bottom, considering Herb for a husband, I wrote this poem.

OR
I could fly from this world's
foot printed sands.
I've jetted away before,
breathed other planets,
the Milky Way's stars
my still-voiced friends.

Or land, feet planted firm
on flawed creviced ground
and share morning dew
and crickets
with you.

THE WEDDING

We held our wedding in Young Israel. Our September 10 wedding day arrived and because the day was on Rosh Hashanah (celebration of the Jewish New Year,) the wedding had to take place after sundown. Driving from our Rego Park apartment, sweat beads dotted Herb's forehead the whole trip. Arriving at the temple, from his jacket pocket, I took out Herb's white handkerchief and dotted off these new beads.

Mom arrived in the car she'd hired for her drive from The Bronx. Her long chartreuse skirt and matching pink and green sheer blouse fitted her form perfectly. Well bejeweled, Mom looked beautiful. We pinned a corsage on her. Sis also looked festive, as did Freddie, when they arrived from their New York apartment. Their happiness glowed.

Friends Aranka and boyfriend Mark and Alan and Glenda arrived. Herb's relatives, especially brother Jerry with Renee', his Uncle Irving with Anna Marie, and his mom poured into the temple. We'd bought a corsage for Herb's mom and pinned it on her.

"Congratulations" Herb and I told her. Anna was beaming and mingling with her family and Dr. Hirschorn, the family doctor who lived across the street from Herb's mom's house.

Guests were standing around the chuppah (the canopy symbolizing God's blessing and protection of the new Jewish home) awaiting the ceremony. The actress always, I stood calm and collected.

Without fanfare, in walked my father, glasses on, in his business suit, with an assistive cane. He'd taken the subway from Queens.

I was so happy to see him. Dad kissed me and Sister. He shook hands with Herb, congratulating him, and with Freddie, as well.

The wedding took place, and afterwards, Dad drew me aside, handing me an envelope.

"I was able to save this much privately, and want you to have it. Betty doesn't know." "Thanks, so much, Dad" I said, and Dad then left for the subway home.

I was so grateful, especially that Dad, alone, could arrive and add his important persona to my wedding. Returning home, I saw that the envelope contained $500. This sum was a nice gift. However, I was more wowed by Dad's being able to attend and his kind gesture of this gift to me and Herb.

The reception dinner took place at the nearby restaurant Herb and I had selected. Jukebox music played. Mom sat next to Anna and the two corsaged ladies had a great time enjoying the celebration. All the rest of the guests did the same.

Herb and I were at last a married couple. There was no honeymoon because we both had work the following day, and I was contending with my recently diagnosed asthma.

REGO PARK APARTMENT

Newly married and still adjusting to our new life, we moved into and furnished our Rego Park apartment, a short walk for me to the train station to the City, and for Herb, his daily drive of close to an hour to his Brooklyn school.

Every morning, we heard our upstairs neighbor open her window, and shout *Deborah*. Then we'd see that bus arrive and call for her daughter.

Same in the afternoons, but in reverse order. At 3:15 the bus would arrive and the daughter, about eight years old, would exit onto the street. The window would open again, *Deborah....,* the upstairs neighbor would yell. The child would call, "Yes, Mom, I'm home. See you soon."

And so it went. We began seeing cockroaches–mostly in the kitchen. Plating our dinners, I'd plate, squash a few–over the stove and some on the floor. I told the super, who sprayed.

We later saw bundles of garbage outside our upstairs neighbor's door.

I knocked, and the door opened. I saw this fat lady, her apron flowing with food stuck on it.

"What do you want?" her bellicose reply.

"Can you please throw your trash bags down the chute? I'm seeing cockroaches in my apartment and think they must be coming from this.

"I'll try," was her answer.

No progress for two days, I called the super.

In a day or two, bags were eliminated and no more cockroaches for me and Herb. He must have sprayed, I figured.

At home, Herb read the paper and worked on his crossword puzzle in the morning. I exercised and took the subway to the City to work.

I'd later come home and make us dinner.

We'd entertain friends. Once, I made a cheese fondue, but the flame got out of control. My hero Herb saved the day!.

One night I made a little wine and cheese party for Herb and me, Sis and Freddie, and friends Gene and Marilyn. We'd all had some wine. Freddie offered some pot, which he'd brought. Herb took a puff and immediately dashed into the bathroom, where he vomited. Gene and Marilyn had a puff or two and could handle it. I puffed and immediately fell asleep on my couch. My vow: from now on, no more pot for Herb or me.

Herb and I didn't have a honeymoon but we went away some weekends to Reiser's Cabins in Schroon Lake NY. Inside the rustic wooden cabin, we enjoyed our little overnight stays and brought food in. It was relaxing and we had a lake in which we swam. So relaxing, that we invited friends Gene and Marilyn to come up and stay overnight with us.

Herb and Gene took their fishing rods, got into a rowboat and began to fish. By the time they arrived back at our cabin, we noticed it was late. Finally entering, they told us, "We were hauled into court: fishing without a permit. We hadn't noticed any sign, but paid the $20 fine." Gene and Marilyn returned to their home happy, but $10 lighter.

Eight

THE MONTCALM RESTAURANT

I had just gotten my driver's license, but Herb, the more seasoned driver, on this rainy night, drove our little green Datsun shift car to Reisers', then The Montcalm Restaurant in Lake George. The Montcalm had a good reputation and we'd heard it was lovely. I had selected it and reserved a table. On the way, the rain grew heavier. We got there. Inside, the large room with Mahogany walls, linen tablecloths and chandeliers was an inviting setting.

"Your table will be ready in a little while. The bar's right over there," the maître d' told us. So we each sat on the blue cushioned seats, on the back wall, liquor bottles in front of the mirrors.

Herb ordered a martini. I had nothing.

After 15 minutes, there was still no table. Herb ordered another, finally consuming his third.

Then, "Mr. and Mrs. Kaufman, your table is ready," the maître 'd called. I stood up, and looked at Herb, who tried to rise from his seat. But the drinks were now swimming in his legs and his head. With a friendly bar patron I helped get Herb to the bathroom, where he promptly threw up. I paid our bill and had the maître' d' wrap our dinners for the ride back to Reiser's.

Inebriated as he was, Herb was in no shape to drive, so it was up to me to get us back. The expression *cats and dogs* was weak for how it was pouring. This put my driving to the test and I drove on the highway–no stop signs–just the torrential downpour–all the way up the 45 minute drive to our Schroon Lake cabin. I did it and was very proud of myself!

Herb's drinks finally out of his system, we exited our car. Proud of me Herb, Herb exclaimed, "You did great, Darling."

Back home, weekdays, after Herb's daily morning orange juice, cereal and crossword puzzles, he'd carpool to school with friends.

I rode my new Cannondale bicycle on an hour-long trip around Oceanside and Hewlett. I figured this exercise was good for my diabetes. On my path in Hewlett, once I had to wait for a gaggle of geese to cross the road. I'd take a quick shower, then catch the train to the City.

BACK HOME

Eventually, we decided a house would be a better investment and followed Herb's brother Jerry and wife Renee', and bought a small ranch house in Oceanside near the railroad station. We could manage with only our green Datsun.

Herb and I frequently went to community concerts, after which we'd meet our friends at a coffee shop and enjoy our sips and munches.

This evening at the Merrick Towne Diner, Herb and I sat with friends waiting for our coffee and...

"Meri," I heard from a woman's voice. It was coming from the front of the diner, near the cashier.

I looked but couldn't find the caller. It didn't take long before another "Meri."

I looked and found this nicely dressed woman, brunette hair in a pageboy style with bangs, walking determinedly right up to our table.

Looking directly at me, the woman, appearing about my age, said, "Meri, don't you remember me?"

I looked into these attractive brown eyes and said, "I'm sorry, but no."

"I'm Brenda," the woman replied. "Your co-counselor from Camp NYDA."

"Oh, my God, I'm so sorry. Of course it's you–only about 20 years after NYDA."

We hugged and kissed and I introduced Herb and she said, "Here's Harvey, now my husband. You remember, from camp, Harvey, don't you? He was the swimming coach."

Of course, we said, and kissed each other.

I invited them to join us and we caught up, learning that Brenda and Harvey lived in Lido Beach. I told her we lived in Oceanside. With our desserts, we said we'd have to get together, and that's what we did.

INSULIN REACTION: RENEE'S HELP

I used the exercise to help control my blood sugars, but then got caught up in this control game. Sugar might rise too high, so I'd ride more. When sugars got low, I'd stop in the nearby 7-11 and buy some junk candy bars to raise my blood sugar. I was spinning in a web of trouble.

One weekend morning, Herb was playing golf with brother Jerry. I got home from a bike ride and was unable to answer the ringing telephone. The next thing I remember was my sister-in-law Renee' at my side on the floor. She was trying to feed me orange juice she'd taken from the refrigerator. This revived me.

Renee' later told me, "Your mom phoned me saying that she'd called you and you sounded funny–not yourself–and asked, could I go over and check on you. And if needed, call for help" she requested.

Renee' continued, "I went right over but didn't have the key with me. So I got to the bathroom window, opened it and climbed in."

I thanked God for my Mom and Renee' and made a note to better control my blood sugars.

BACK HOME: SHOWS

Both of us enjoying theater back home, we Kaufmans attended local shows and met friends at local diners for coffee. Posters decorated coffee shop walls. They publicized auditions for little theatrical shows being presented at community theater locations. My love of acting persisted. I auditioned and got the part of the mother in the Sholem Aleichem show *Gymnasium (The High School)*.

I learned my lines while commuting, by reading my script page by page and over and over. I got good reactions to my performance and after the show, in the car, Herb handed me a little gift box which, when I opened it, revealed a 14 karat Jewish star and chain. I was so thrilled that my darling surprised me with this gift–so appropriate to the show, as well as beautiful and thoughtful.

Next, in the nearby town of Baldwin I auditioned for, and got the role of Edna, the wife in Neil Simon's *The Prisoner of Second Avenue*, an excellent and very popular Neil Simon comedy.

This was very exciting and I received a good reception for my acting. I invited most of our friends to come and enjoy the show, and even my boss, Bernie Ilson, who attended with wife Carol.

After the show, Herb, before we arrived at the coffee shop, presented handed me another little gift–a wrapped box. Inside I found a 14 karat gold tennis-style bracelet with a number of stones embedded. I couldn't identify these colored beauties till the next day when we went to the jeweler.

In the store studded with contemporary and antique and estate jewelry, "They're cabochon stones," the jeweler told us.

I was so thrilled that my darling had once again showed his appreciation with this thoughtful gift and the beautiful congratulations card he'd created. Like all these "gift-times" I grabbed my darling and gave him a big hug and kiss, and again, my thanks for his thoughtfulness!

In Oceanside, I appeared in the chorus of *Mame*, and sang and danced my heart out–and loved doing it.

For *The Diary of Anne Frank* in Lindenhurst, I was cast as Mrs. Frank. For this role, I had to rehearse about 6 nights a week. That meant, returning from work and making the 40 minute drive to and from Lindenhurst. Toward the end of rehearsals, I became very sick and had to drop out.

NEXT AVOCATION: POETRY WRITING

What would my new vocation be? Poetry writing? No harm trying I thought. So I took a workshop in Freeport, contributed my poems and listened to work of other poets. I felt I wanted to learn more.

I was working in the City and learned about The Poetry Society of America. Its members included my favorite poet, Edna St. Vincent Millay, and also Carl Sandburg and Robert Frost. To be accepted, one had to submit 10 poems in four sets–that meant for the four judges to read and vote on. I selected my best and I mailed them off and waited for an answer. Every day, I ran to our mailbox and looked for either a letter of acceptance or rejection.

Happily, one day it came. The letter stated that I'd been accepted. It gave me a list of advantages, including the opportunity to join their Peer Workshop. And so began, after work, my Tuesday night treks downtown to the National Arts Club, where the PSA met.

I brought in and read a poem which was severely criticized. Dejected, I went out to the bathroom and cried out a storm...and then I returned. In the weeks that followed, some of my poems gained approval, which made me happy.

Here I learned to take the criticism from where it came and I became less sensitive to the criticisms. Many of the poets offered good ideas on how I could strengthen my poem and particular lines.

From the workshop, I'd go home and find time to create. Mornings, after the railroad, walking to work up Avenue of the Americas, I'd think of ideas, and later, jot these ideas down and develop them.

And I tried to get my works published. This meant, in my spare time, looking up journals, making copies and sending the poems off to this one and that–a lot of paper and postage.

Many got rejected. However, I got several works published, including my poem *TRAINMAN*. The Long Island College journal C W Post ran a competition and it published my poem and awarded me Second Prize. I was thrilled with my accomplishment..

The poem reads as follows:

TRAINMAN

Body young, muscled,
belted with a railroad buckle.

Mustache
over a Mediterranean smile.
Licorice hair –
rebellion length
under a conductor's cap.

"Tickets please, all tickets" –
his mild morning call,
easing down the aisle
perfumed with rising coffee vapors,
attache case leather,
newsprint.

MERILEE KAUFMAN

Leaning over seats of two's, three's,
checking commuter tickets,
punching day trippers,
eyes shiny,
brown like old tootsie pops.

As our train huffed into the station,
over the address system
he'd read the Ching Chow comics.

Gone several years,
he's returned
and punches my ticket again.

Still the lean body,
railroad buckle, leather card pouch,
jangle of keys;

mustache tracking across his face,
indented by
ticket-taking years;

shining eyes.

But now
short hair
salted

and no more
Ching Chow.

Also, the PSA invited me to read in one of their readings of Peer Group members. Of course, I invited Herb and his brother Jerry. I felt nervous to read, but happy and proud to be part of this esteemed group.

HERB'S 40TH SURPRISE PARTY

In 1976, Herb turned 40 years old. With our friends, I decided to throw him a surprise birthday party . With a great deal of humor, several talented friends wrote a script based on Herb's life. This had to be rehearsed.

I told Herb I had to stay late and work. Commuting towards home, I took the railroad to the East Rockaway stop, where my dear friend Geri Homelsky picked me up and took me back to her home nearby.

Here, Herb's colleagues had assembled to go over the script which they would read at the party. For accuracy, I checked dates and added events. Rehearsal complete, Geri drove me home, and my mini-lies to Herb continued.

The night of the party, I told Herb we were going to the home of Geri and her husband Les for dinner. We'd bought the wine, and I felt like I was leading the lamb to slaughter.

Les opened the door and friends throughout Herb's life and our life greeted us, hollering a great big SURPRISE!!! Herb's forehead dotted immediately with great sweat beads as his mouth and eyes opened wide. We supported his back so he didn't fall from the shock, and we headed in and greeted all our friends. Herb's brother Jerry and our sister-in-law Renee' were there too.

After reading the script, and Herb opening his cards and presents, Geri brought out coffee and the beautiful cake she'd created. With frosting of vanilla and chocolate square boxes, it mimicked the crossword puzzles Herb loved and indulged in.

We chatted with everyone and on the way home, recovering from his initial shock, Herb, with a smile on his face, warned me: "Don't ever do this to me, again!" Arriving home, we kissed and laughed more about this terrific event.

MY WRITING

My high school English teacher once said to me, "You write well. I think you'll make a good reporter."

I needed to write–for myself. While I was working at Bernie's, at lunchtime I'd go around the neighborhood. Lunching at a Health Salad type restaurant which I enjoyed a lot, I thought I'd like to write a review, and asked the owner if he wanted this. "Sure," he jumped at this chance.

My publication had a small circulation, but Manny, the restaurant's owner, was thrilled to see the glowing review in print. He had it copied and pasted it on his window. My superlatives infusing this review, potential diners could not resist. Herb and I enjoyed the many restaurant offerings–for free.

Not one to let a food-opportunity go to waste. I contacted several other restaurants and with managers' permissions, and Herb accompanying me, sampled fare at a wide range of restaurants from countries like India, China, Mexico and more. For me with my diabetes, and for Herb, I watched what we ate. We had a good time, to which my scrapbook of reviews attests.

VALLEYS AND MOUNTAINS

One restaurant I got to review was the well-known Peng's Chinese Restaurant in New York's East 40's.

As our Moo Goo Gai Pan, Chicken Chow Mein and spring rolls were being placed on our table, who, accompanied by an escort, should enter? None other than our U.S. Secretary of State Henry Kissinger!

Herb asked: "When he sits, should I ask for an autograph?"

"No," I replied. "Let the man eat his dinner in peace"

"So we continued our delicious meal at this highly rated restaurant and I wrote a glowing review.

I also explored my interests. Oil lamps was one and, after research, the article I wrote was published in the New York Daily News Sunday Magazine. The Magazine also published my feature revealing the beautiful antiques adorning the home of Herb's cousin.

This was in addition to a little article I wrote on Jerusalem artichokes, als0 published in the News.

Then, through my job, with my business show business connections, I knew how to reach managers, and wrote articles, based on the interviews I'd arranged with celebrities Joel Grey, Beverly Sills, Smokey Robinson, Roberta Flack and more.

In 1983 I was about to turn 40 years old. With my diabetes, I never expected to live that long, and decided to throw a party. That's what we did–at the Ship's Inn in East Rockaway. Together Herb and I planned and made invitations and place settings, chose the menu, invited guests and enjoyed seeing the many friends and relatives who showed up.

MERILEE KAUFMAN

Merilee and Herb at a party

1993

1993 had two major events. First, I left the PR job I'd held for 23 years.

It was a small office and there was nowhere else I could go. Bernie, now concerned with grandchildren, was holding onto the company money. So I decided to leave and open my own business, which I did in the basement of our home.

It was now June and I'd wanted to celebrate my 50th birthday. Herb and I were in the middle of planning.

Next, we got, in the mail, an invitation from friend Geri to attend her daughter Jody's engagement party. It would be at McQuade's, a local bar and restaurant in Island Park.

It was local, so I didn't think I needed to get dressed too fancy. That day, however, Herb convinced me that I should look very good. I chose a new pink dress I'd purchased, I put on makeup and fixed my hair. Then, for my diabetes, I phoned the restaurant to see what the menu would be.

"I'd like to know the menu for the party lunchtime for Jody Homelsky," I said. Pause.

"Sorry, Miss, but we have no party for Jody Homelsky."

I persevered: "You must. We have our invitations..." and I read him the invitation.

"I'm sorry, Miss. We have no such party."

"Well," I said to Herb. "We'll try the McQuade's in nearby Rockville Centre. I did, and got the same answer.

I said, let's try the Island Park branch again. At that point, which was near the appointed time to be at McQuade's, Island Park, with Herb getting nervous, my demure husband said to me, "Let me have the phone." I phoned the number on the invitation, gave the to Herb, and his conversation went like this:

"Hi, my wife called awhile ago asking about the Homelsky Party. Oh, you found the reservation. Okay, thanks. And the foods you're serving? Oh, yes, chicken, meatballs, salads, fruits, vegetables, soda, coffee, tea and cake." Herb told me this with a straight face, and I agreed it was fine.

We drove in, parked, opened the door, and we were met with a huge "SURPRISE!" My turn! I was shocked that Herb pulled this off! Of course, he had the assistance of Renee'. Wow, my husband's thespian talents on the phone amazed me! I learned later that he'd held the button down so no call took place.

MERILEE KAUFMAN

At Merilee's 50th Birthday Surprise Party: Les, Herb, Geri and Merilee pause their joy for a photo

Jukebox was running and Herb and I circulated. Friends were shooting loads of photos and at the door, and in walked my mom. At Herb's secret invitation, she'd taken a cab from her Bronx home and showed up. I was thrilled to see her here. Of course, that meant she'd stay over at our house and the next day, we'd drive her home.

Our friend Stan, with a great sense of humor, read a very funny tribute to me, and Stan's wife Gloria went around with her camera, taking photos of guests. A few weeks later, Gloria gave me a beautiful album of my party. Friend Les also said fond remembrances. Then my mom took the microphone, adding her very sweet praise and happiness.

It was a wonderful celebration. At the end, Herb and I took more photos with Mom on the deck of our home, and then we dined on some of the leftovers we'd brought home.

When mom went to sleep, Herb took out a box with a curly ribbon tying it closed. I opened it and found a gorgeous 14K necklace with scarabs of different colors arranged on it.

"For your 50th birthday, I didn't want to make a scene in front of people," said my sweetheart.

I couldn't have been more happy! However, I didn't really love it and gently shared.

"Herb, darling, once again, you've done a beautiful thing. But you wanna know something???"

"You don't love it," Herb jumped in. "No problem," said my adoring Herb. "Okay, tomorrow we'll go to R & K Jewelers and exchange it."

We did and I selected this gorgeous choker of 14 karat gold on one side, and on the other, silver gold.

I couldn't have been happier, and Herb was so delighted he could do this for me!

Ten

TRAVELS

In the seventies we visited Spain, Italy and England.

SPAIN

Near Seville, we visited Italica, an ancient Roman city, close to the town of Santiponce. We stopped to look in their cemetery and had the good luck of being shown around by a very elderly groundskeeper. My little knowledge of Spanish allowed me to converse with this man and understand and translate for Herb, at my side. Herb, good at language, tried to speak in the bits and pieces of Spanish that he knew and could understand from my translations.

In his gray uniform including a cap this attendant wore to protect him from the sun and 90 degree weather, this little man, with many teeth missing, seemed happy to share his knowledge.

In museums of Madrid, we saw paintings by Picasso, Goya, Miro and Velasquez, among others.

In restaurants, we frequently enjoyed paella and their hake, a good Spanish white fish.

We visited Granada, Andalusia, and Cordoba, home of Moses ben Maimon, commonly known as Maimonides and also referred to by the acronym Rambam. Maimonides was a Sephardic Jewish philosopher who became one of the most prolific and influential Torah scholars of the Middle Ages.

The Alhambra, in Granada, Andalucia, was the famous palace and fortress complex. It is one of the most renowned monuments of Islamic architecture. I remember water continually flowing in the palace pools. This sound was supposed to be calming–and it was, as was the whole day until the night, until....

In our hotel room, I stayed up all night because my blood sugar was descending. I checked it frequently to make sure I did not go into insulin shock from too low a blood sugar. I figured that whether I had taken too much insulin for a meal or the body considered our tour-walking too much exercise, the result was my blood sugar dropping.

Herb knew that I knew how to treat this, so he went to sleep–but with one eye open.

I always carried bottles and packages of glucose to raise the blood glucose. That night they came in handy.

LONDON

In London, we toured The British Museum. At The Royal Albert Concert Hall, one of London's two largest, we heard an excellent concert of music by Andres Segovia, the Spanish guitarist. We enjoyed the restaurants. At one cafe, we met a lovely couple, whose accent we admired. We learned they were from South Africa. Addresses were exchanged and we said we'd keep in touch.

On all our European trips, before we took off, I wanted to meet the Captains–I so I could feel sure they were competent to fly and did not look like they were on drugs, which in hindsight does sound a little hilarious even to me!

ITALY

On our flight to Italy, after meeting Captain Palermo, I sat and tested my blood sugar. It was low. I treated this and my anxiety was relieved. Living taught me that low blood sugar can cause feelings of anxiety and fear.

In Italy we were cautious of pickpockets who we'd been warned, covered the place quite well. I held tight my handbag which, I'd been told, might be stolen, and we were careful not to step on syringes discarded by drug users.

Italy was a beautiful trip with bus tours through mountains and seeing the multitudes of olive trees and with our tour group, trying great restaurants and cafes. Restaurants, we learned, were composed of big breakfasts, light lunches and minimal dinners. All the foods were great, and again, I had to try and control my carbohydrates.

We went to museums, enjoyed siestas and had many dinners out.

In Rome, we climbed the Spanish Steps–138 in all. We visited the Murano glass factory, where we purchased gifts of jewelry and exquisite pottery.

In Venice, a romantic interlude was our gondola experience. We were serenaded by gondoliers crooning love songs "Inamorata," "That's Amore" and many others. Herb and I both loved this musicacle.

Here, we walked across a bridge where vendors sold their jewelry and pottery. Herb bought me a beautiful 14K ring whose black onyx oval face boasted a peaceful white dove.

Herb particularly enjoyed seeing the magnificent sculptures and paintings by Leonardo DaVinci, particularly the Mona Lisa and The Last Supper.

We saw St. Peter's Basilica, the Sistine Chapel, Trevi Fountain and The Vatican. At Plaza San Marco we were greeted by a multitude of pigeons converging, squatting and searching for food.

BERKSHIRES

Closer to home vacations took us to The Berkshire Mountains in Massachusetts. We'd learned that they had terrific theatrical programs, good museums, as well as good restaurants and golf courses.

The Berkshires Chamber of Commerce recommended the Oak and Spruce Resort in South Lee. For a few years we stayed in their Hotel. Then their manager approached us with his selling spiel.

With his firm build and brown hair, this 30-ish year old man in shorts and khaki green shirt said, "Because you're such good customers, we can offer you a deal to buy one of our new time-share units that we're building now.

Viewing the model, we saw that in their individual kitchens, we'd be able to refrigerate our shopping and make our meals too. We had a parking spot and there was a nice pool, as well. I could enjoy my swimming exercise, and Herb could play golf in the resort's golf course.

We were close to other golf courses, as well. And we had enough space, in our unit, to invite friends up for overnights.

We could meet the cost and, we thought, the annual maintenance fee.

We considered all and decided to take it.

For dinners we went into town and selected a restaurant at which to dine.

We shot photos, took walks, saw many shows, including the glorious concert palace, Tanglewood. Here, under a shed, we enjoyed great concerts and bumped into people we knew from New York.

Mornings we'd walk to the local coffee and newspaper store. Herb picked up our NY Times and I, my Green Mountain decaf coffee.

We played ping pong and backgammon. Herb golfed and I did my walking and swimming exercise. Sometimes, at night, we'd do karaoke. You can guess who sang.

I wore my new gold tennis bracelet into the pool. Cleaning up and showering later, I noticed the bracelet was gone. Oh, my God! My new tennis bracelet–gift from Herb–gone. Oh, dear. Oh, dear!!!

I phoned the front desk. "I just returned from swimming," I told this man, "and lost my new 14K tennis bracelet with colored stones. Has it been turned in?" I asked.

"Not yet, but we'll keep our eyes out and ears open for you. And your unit is what number?"

I told him, and waited.

I was really down, but in about an hour the phone rang.

"Hello, Mrs. Kaufman. This is the front desk clerk. Did you lose a 14K bracelet today?"

"God, yes–in the pool, I believe," I answered. "Was it found?"

"Yes, I have it here, so please come up and I'll give it to you."

"Right-o," I replied. "I'll be right there."

I got it and all was well. I figured that, returning home, I'd have the jeweler attach a second lock to the clasp.

GUESTS

Marcia and Gerry drove up and filled our refrigerator with loads of farm-bought apples, oranges, grapes, pears and a bottle of Merlot wine. Together, we played Scrabble and some of the games they brought up, enjoyed the swimming pool and karaoke at night.

We bought our tickets for the theaters and Jacob's Pillow (the noted dance company,) and Herb with Gerry, bought admissions to golf.

Another time, Jerry and Renee' came up. Activities were theater, fine dining, shopping for Renee' and me and golf for the men.

Good theater was a special treat. One summer, during an intermission, I saw, and said hello to actor Chris Noth of *Law and Order* fame. Another time, we spotted, and said hello to actor James Naughton.

In a ladies room, Joanne Woodward entered the stall next to mine and I could hear her pee. Many of these actors came to appear in shows and several, to see fellow actors appear in productions.

We dined one night at The Orchard–a very elegant and classy restaurant. Fresh flowers adorned our table and waiters served their stations wearing tuxedos. Across the room, we spotted actor Paul Newman chatting.

Another evening at dinner, after splitting a full bottle of Merlot, Herb and I proceeded to the theater and sat in the second row orchestra for *All My Sons*. The Arthur Miller drama. Actor James Naughton, was walking back and forth across the stage performing his lines. Despite Herb's continual nudging, I fell asleep.

Eleven

HEART DISEASE

On this particular morning, towards the end of our stay, returning from my exercise walk to our unit, I felt pain in my back. Continuing my walk, the pain persisted. By the time I reached and stepped onto our lawn, I collapsed.

Neighbors knocked on our door and Herb came out. He and the neighbor picked me up and helped me walk inside. That's when Herb phoned our physician in New York.

"As soon as possible," he told us, "get her into my office."

Happily we were finishing our vacation week, so we got our things together and left for our home and the doctor's office nearby. After the exam and EKG, our internist said "Your heart is irregular. Get to the office of Dr. Richard Horowitz."

Dr. Mailloux phoned for an appointment for me. As the cardiologist finished with the preliminary exam, the verdict was out. I was diagnosed with heart disease.

VALLEYS AND MOUNTAINS

Dr. Horowitz picked up his phone and asked for an appointment for me with Dr. Jerome Zisfein. "You'll need an angiogram," he told me, and a stent to let blood flow into your arteries.

"Go over to the hospital now, if you can."

That's what Herb and I did. We went directly into the hospital's heart unit.

Nurses made me comfortable. An hour or so later Dr. Zisfein arrived, greeted me and told me not to worry. It won't hurt and will take a short time to heal. "But you'll have to rest overnight here until the stent settles," he told me.

Okay, Herb left, returning with my Michael Connelly book. Jerry and Renee' arrived, too, and told me not to worry.

I now had coronary artery disease and a stent.

Next morning I felt fine, but had been instructed not to go down stairs for about a week. Also, I had to wait about a week till I could do my exercise-walk near our home.

I said goodbye to the nurses. Walking toward the floor's exit, Dr. Lomasky, my endocrinologist, came bopping along.

"I wanted to wish you luck," he told me. I was so happy I kissed his cheek, hugged him thanked him for this visit.

An attendant took me downstairs, awaiting, with me, our car. In moments our gray Camry Corolla pulled up and Herb got out to help me. I hugged and kissed him, and I thanked the attendant.

I was so thrilled to see my darling Herb–my sweetheart and my life saver–and entered the car for our drive home.

Summer after summer, we returned to our timeshare unit, until rising maintenance fees became ridiculous. We put our unit up for sale. No buyers. After many enjoyable years there, we took a total loss, but were glad to be free of that cost.

BERKSHIRES TO HOME–THE DRIVE

2014

The roads to and from The Berkshires were curvy. On the way home from our last trip up there, we hit a terrible rain storm–all the way. With me at his side navigating, Herb did a great job driving and got us home safely.

TRAVELS CLOSER TO HOME

We went down to West Virginia and attended a fair recreating the 1700's. Their participants went around dressed in costumes of the time, we visited homes and dined at a few of the restaurants taking part. All waiters were dressed in 1700's attire and we ordered foods popular at the time such as fricassees of various meats with herbs, and sometimes a good amount of claret.

We also ordered common food among the lower classes, such as corn porridge or mush, or hominy with greens and salt-cured meat. Occasionally, in the local restaurants we enjoyed the traditional southern fried chicken and chitlins.

At one of their amusement parks we got in one of the cars that ride up and swing quite a bit. I got terribly scared, and screamed. Herb called to the attendant, who stopped the ride. I got off, but brave Herb stayed on and enjoyed it.

In the States, we traveled to New Orleans. In one of their recommended restaurants, in the bathroom, taking my pre-dinner insulin injection, I accidentally dropped my vial of insulin on the tile floor. It broke and we had to leave and drive to a pharmacy for replacement. We returned to the restaurant, I took my shot and we enjoyed our oysters Rockefeller, chicken gumbo, jambalaya, rice and beans, bananas Foster and beignets with their smokey and nutty coffee flavor.

And I discovered that what would have prevented a broken insulin vial was, when opening a new vial, wrapping a large piece of clear packing tape around it–so if it fell to the floor, it would be cushioned. This worked for me, so I wrote in and sent it to one of the magazines for people with diabetes. They published it, and I was happy that my recommendation had been well received.

Twelve

FASHION SHOWS

We'd become members of Temple Avodah. Prior to 1986, I had modeled in several Temple Dinner and Fashion Shows. Under my mother's influence, I always loved clothes and dressing up. For these shows I had to go to the boutique and select three outfits I liked and that looked good on me. That meant cinched waists and showing no belly. Then, from my collection, at home, I had to find matching shoes. I took pleasure in this process, and especially seeing myself all beautified amid the temple mirrors and cameras flashing.

At Temple Fashion Show, "the three "M's": Marilyn, Merilee and Marcia pause for a photo.

The hostess, to the dining women, for example, would say, "And now, we have Merilee in this beautiful kelly green colored gown with green emeralds studding the bodice. Doesn't she look gorgeous?" and the applause would be great. I enjoyed the attention from the introductions and walking the gangplank.

Radiating joy, Merilee, in shiney red satin gown waves to attendees at Temple Avodah fashion show

Aglow, in her kelly green gown, Merilee parades down the aisle at Temple Avodah's Fashion Show.

BEFORE PARKINSONS DISEASE

During our married life, Herb was active. Of course, we both worked. For fun, we'd play tennis with Stan and Gloria, poker with Les and Geri, and we danced–at the Community Center and at Kusher's Country Club in the Borscht Belt.

Herb thought he was a good dancer and I let him hold that belief. He could hold me and move to the beat and spin me out so I could whirl around. I didn't think Herb was that good a dancer. However, we could dance together on the floor, and I had a partner who loved me and that was good enough for me.

Herb adored playing golf, which his Uncle Bernie had taught him. Herb taught this to Jerry and nephew Sean, as well. Weekends, every spring and summer day, he'd get up early, breakfast and be off to the golf course–with Jerry, friend Norman or by himself. He also entered lots of golf tournaments and while he came back always saying he wasn't good enough, he had a good time.

MOM INTO THE GRANDELL

From someone you loved, did you ever have to remove something they treasured. I did? That's what me, and my sister had to do with our mom. Mom was in her upper 80's and living alone in her Bronx apartment for some seventy odd years–that's since she was married.

One of Mom's neighbors, the doctor in the adjacent first floor apartment, called me.

"Your mom, Sylvia," she began, "had been acting strangely and seemed overly fearful. She told me that, "...from her open door open, she could see that a man came into the building and, she said, "I thought he was going to hurt me."

The doc continued. "I think you should come up and look in on her."

I thanked this doc and that's what Herb and I did.

We met Mom. In her short sleeved blouse, skirt and sandals, her cheeks rouged, she looked fine. We said "Hi" and kissed hello.

Mom then told us: "I saw this man–first, in the building lobby and then, in my apartment."

Herb and I called a rabbi whom Mom had confidence in. He came over and spoke to Mom. Realizing something was wrong, he suggested we call Montefiore Hospital's Emergency Department. We did and they sent over an EMT who examined and spoke to Mom. "You'd better get her over to the hospital's Emergency Room," the young Hispanic looking man told us.

He's in this business, I realized, so I figured, so we could trust him. In the EMT car, we all went.

In the ER, within the cold chrome and glass windows, the hospital doc took blood and spoke to her. "How are you feeling, dear lady? " the young doctor asked.

"I'm as fine as you," Mom quipped.

"Then I guess you can leave," the doc continued.

However, then the bloodwork came back and he said, "No, dear. Your sodium level is very low and we need to do more testing. Let's get you checked in." We filled out the forms and made sure that Mom got fed.

Mom had gone to her internist every couple of weeks. How could he overlook the low sodium!? I'd investigate later, I thought.

The nurse hydrated Mom with an IV and glasses of water and juice. '"This will replenish your sodium," she told Mom.

The social worker then spoke to us. "You know that your Mom's living alone is dangerous. I suggest that either you, or your sister, take her to live with you."

With our work schedules and our difficult relationships with Mom, neither I nor Sis could do this. Next step: a nursing home. I shared all this with Sis and she was gung-ho on the nursing home idea. Our friend

Bette, who wrote a book about nursing homes, briefed us on what to look for–urine smell and trash bins chock full.

Meanwhile, I called mom's doctor's office and asked about Mom's sodium levels on the last few tests. Dr. Gaynor's secretary told us that, for weeks, they all revealed low sodium levels. I asked to speak to Dr. Gaynor "He's on vacation" the secretary said. I was furious, and fumed as I shared this with Herb.

A short while later, we got a call from Dr. Gaynor's associate, a physician, who told us, "The secretary should never have revealed these results. Dr. Gaynor will be back next week you can speak with him." This did not calm me. I tamed my fuming, later contemplating what I'd do.

After surveying the nursing home scene, Herb and I discovered several which smelled of urine and whose trash bins were overflowing. Finally, we placed Mom in The Grandell Center for Nursing and Rehabilitation in nearby Long Beach. Bette had placed her mom there and she did pretty well. Mom was pretty much recovered, but to get her there, we created a mini-lie.

"Mom, Dear, we're going to drive you to a place where you can rest for a while, and be taken care of." Calmly, she agreed and the social worker made the call and we got her into the ambulette. Herb followed in our car.

THE GRANDELL

Mom was placed in a semi-private room, facing the parking lot. Without the lights on it was dingy looking. However, lighting revealed paintings of simple street scenes of places that might have been Paris or Venice.

Mom's room-mate, Anna, we were told, had dementia. At night, decrepit-looking little white-haired Anna would silently take Mom's outfits from the closet and walk them down to the nursing station. Several items of Moms got lost and then found again.

Sis was in the City and busy with her full-time secretarial job and part-time antiques business. I was on scene, so I had to take care of things. And Mom was quite upset and vented her anger at me.

"Why did you do this to me!?" she wanted to know. "Where are all my things–my clothes and personal items–my jewelry, handbags and money!?"

"Mom, we'll be taking care of things for you now. In time, I'll bring what I can from your apartment." This put Mom at ease, for a while, but also I tried to encourage her to be charitable.I told her, "All these patients don't have the brain power you still have."

Mom was feeling very down. The social worker spoke to her. Eventually, Mom was placed on an anti-anxiety drug.

This social worker, Eileen, blonde haired and stout, when I saw her outside, smoked heavily. She listened carefully and suggested to Mom that she meet with me and share her feelings.

We met. "I feel dumped and abandoned," Mom said. "You don't want me. Elaine doesn't want me. You're discarding me."

I told her, "You, like all of us, are aging. You, living alone in your apartment, can no longer handle the shopping and cleaning.

"Elaine and I both still love you loads and need you to be well. I've checked and found that The Grandell, near our home, is accessible by railroad to me and Sis (coming from New York,) is the best place. Also, it's nearby and close to the Boardwalk, which I think you'll like. We can take you for walks there. It's a lively place.

I told her that I'd visit her often and Sis, when she could.

Reiterating, "Mom, we are in no-way dumping or abandoning you. We love you and, as we all age, we're seeking the best."

Her pain eased and we hugged and kissed and confirmed that we loved each other.

"I'll see you soon, I assured her. "And, also, Mom, they have a beauty parlor," I pointed out.

"And the nearby Long Beach Library has music programs. I'll take you," I suggested to Mom.

MUSIC

I took Mom to the Long Beach Library for several music programs I thought she'd enjoy. We saw singers who were pretty good, playing with trios and quartets.

"Taking piano lessons, growing up," Mom had told Sis and me, "my teacher, Mr. Gumbatz, told me he thought I could be a concert pianist. However, the Depression hit and our family needed money, so my piano lessons had to be discontinued."

Mom, years ago, had gifted me and Herb with money to buy a piano.

With music now in my head, and no experience buying a piano, our wall dimensions on a white piece of paper in my pocket, I railroaded to Macy's Herald Square. Here, I spoke to salesmen, and selected a maple-colored Hardman-Peck console piano.

In my junior high school, I was in a glee club and always loved music. I thought with my knowledge of music and my dramatic training, I, too, could perform at libraries. All I'd need was an accompanist.

I had a friend Judy Feldman, Program Director of the Oceanside Library. Judy was a tiny sparrow-like woman, who appeared nervous when she introduced programs before audiences. We lunched and I told Judy that I'd like to create and sing in music programs–at the Oceanside Library and other libraries. I asked if she knew of a pianist who might accompany me. She suggested Paul Guariglia. I invited him over.

Long gray-haired Paul was tall, skinny, with a big hook nose. He was polite. He played the piano, and I showed Paul some of my singing and proposed we make a duet. He was agreeable.

So began my side career of booking libraries and singing in programs I'd created. We'd be called *Ivories and Melodies*, I had decided.

I'd write pitch letters and, on the phone, call and sell this to library program directors. Dates scheduled, I arranged for Paul and I to get together. We'd plow through the 30's and 40's the music I'd collected and I'd compile programs.We'd rehearse about two or three times.

After each rehearsal Paul, about 40 years old, would ask "Could you spare some food, please". I gave him what I had: grapes, cherries, and he was happy. This filled in his very spare frame. I'd get directions for the libraries and Paul would drive us.

Paul used these gigs to plug his personal solo programs. At intermissions, he'd mention where and when he was playing his concerts. I needed him and this helped him so I didn't mind.

With library program directors, I negotiated fees, and after concerts. I gave Paul his share.

Paul and I recorded a disc to send to libraries for them to hear and decide if they wanted us.

After about six years of our dueting, on a very hot summer day, I thought we would skip the intermission and go right through. I asked the audience if they agreed. They did.

Paul played the remaining pieces, but he was very angry, I could tell, because, to his mind, I'm sure, he could not promote his shows.That meant he'd lose his business.

At show's end, in front of the remaining audience, he yelled at me–and I was very embarrassed. This was totally unprofessional, I thought, and told him so. I decided that was the last show I'd do with him.

After about six weeks, Paul phoned. "I'm sorry, Merilee, for the way I behaved at our last concert. You see, I had to play a mass and was late. I should never have spoken to that way–especially in front of the audience."

I thanked him and said goodbye.

END SINGING WITH PAUL

In our apartment, speaking to Sis on our phone, I said, "Sis, you know I've been performing at libraries, right?

"Yes," she said. "I'd love to hear you."

"How about I play you our CD?"

"I'd love that," she told me.

And so I played it and Sis was overjoyed. "Freddie," she called. "Come here and listen to Meri singing like she does at her shows."

Freddie followed directions and drew nearer to listen.

"That's wonderful," Sis told me.

"Very nice," Meri, Freddie agreed.

I was now an experienced professional singer. Friend Judy who, like me, loved music, told me of a pianist/singer named Frank O'Brien. With his bassist Vinnie Ciaravolo, Frank headlined at local restaurants.

Merilee singing with bassist Vinnie Ciaravolo at Tavolo's Restaurant

So, we found the *Cala Di Mare* restaurant in Rockville Centre. Herb and I met Judy and her husband Len and dined, and enjoyed the terrific music, and even danced. In between numbers, Judy mentioned to Frank that I sang and he invited me up. I went up, told him the song, my key and rhythm, and sang. The diners applauded and I felt like a star.

We followed Frank to many other restaurants. I always prepped a song or two, and had a wonderful time listening to, and making, music.

SUPERSTORM SANDY

It was 2012 and we were hit by Superstorm Sandy. Our home was in a high flood area. Fortunately, a snow-bird friend, in Florida, invited us to stay in her Meadowbrook condo. A good thing. When we returned, we found about 3 feet of water in our basement.

Prior to this storm, the carpenter Herb had contracted to build shelves in our basement. They were now chock full with foods I'd stocked. All, except the coffee cans and detergent bottles, would have to be discarded. In the basement, our washer and dryer would have to be replaced and the house would need to be completely dried. A restoration company did this.

Thirteen

AGING

We realized also that as we aged, and walking down the stairs and up, carrying food and the wash and laundry detergent and soda bottles was too much. We needed to move out. So began our search for a coop or condo.

PARKINSON'S

Going out with friends to dinner or a show, several, including Renee', noted that Herb walked with a shuffle and suggested I get him to a doctor. Our internist told us, "I think you've got to see a neurologist."

After numerous neurological tests, Dr. Jeret told us, "You've got Parkinson's Disease." And looking at me, "and you are the caregiver."

This physician prescribed some medications and we made an appointment to return in 4 months.

"Caregiver," I thought. I've never been a mother or taken care of a sick person, except for our colds, after one of which I wrote this poem:

SICK TOGETHER

My wheeze answers his dry hack.
He chills. I bear-hug,
raise thermostat.
Clammy, we kick covers.

Sneezes ring staccato.
Crumpled tissues, mucus-moist,
snowflake the carpet.

Cleanse thermometer.
Monitor digital temperatures,
plummeting, ascending, plummeting –
a stock market gone wild –

swimming in teas, soups,
humidifier humming.

Published in the *New York Times Living column*

So what did "caregiver" mean? I wondered. I'd soon find out.

"What's the leading cause of death from Parkinson's?" I asked the neurologist.

"Falling, and breaking bones and hitting one's head," Dr. Jeret told us.

That was the beginning of our nine-year Parkinson's journey.

After the doc's diagnosis, we stopped at the diner. I thought Herb was holding up fairly well–no tears. He told me over his pancake lunch: "I always wondered what illness would take me. I hope you'll be able to handle me when things get rough."

Reaching to hold his hand, I replied, "My darling, I love you and will do my very best. And when we need help, we'll get it. Please don't worry about this. I'll be here to help you continue doing what you love. We'll enjoy our friends, tv, films, good food, and all that we can.

When his lunch came, Herb dug into it.

Herb was 78 years old and I was 71.

RVC COOP

A terrific real estate agent, Marlene Gross, hunted for us, showing us a few properties. She found us a great coop in Rockville Centre–at a super location. This was close enough to Herb's brother and Renee's home, which had been a consideration. It was also within walking distance for me to the Long Island Railroad, on which I'd need to commute to my City job.

We had our own parking spot (for which we'd pay) and a laundry and trash room right on our floor. What also sold us, particularly me, was that the apartment included numerous huge closets. Our home was shown, offers made, and we finally agreed on a deal.

DONATE FURNITURE TO ISLAND PARK CHURCH

Our purchase deal included our holding onto much of the beautiful furniture left in this new apartment. Therefore, we'd need to sell our precious big antique furniture from our Oceanside home.

I'd located this church in nearby Island Park. It held fairs every weekend and sold loads of furniture. They had a truck and several young men who volunteered for the church. A date and time was arranged and these kind college students arrived and carried out our huge bedroom bureau, chests, armoire, night tables and coffee table. G O N E and emptier, our home.

YARD SALE

We contracted Tom, the person friend Geri hired for her sale. Over the next two days we put on our lawns sheets, pillowcases, pillows, furniture, about 20 toothpaste tubes, perhaps 10 hair blowers, two Cannondale racers, and my Schwinn exercise bike.

This helped me realize what a hoarder I was. We also sold my precious nutria coat that I saw in a furrier while in New York, walking down Seventh Avenue. I paid $750 for this with the money I earned from one of my feature articles.

We continued carrying out and placing radios, a TV, jewelry and paintings. Friends and neighbors came and helped, watching the "lookers" and buying for themselves, as well. We gave away a lot, including to our neighbors across the street, the Oak dining table and chairs we'd bought at an upstate auction.

Folks wanted to see the bed and night tables. To prevent theft, accompanied by one of our friends, shoppers paraded through the house, viewing and buying our bed, night tables and some paintings. We figured that, until our move, we could sleep on our living room couch and lounge chairs.

We did well. grossing about $2,000 and gave half to Tom, who was very grateful. I also gave him a theatrical sword from the Broadway show I worked on: *Her First Roman.*

"Thank you so much," Tom told us. "My son collects swords and he'll like this."

There was clothing to get rid of. We tackled Herb's first. He kept most of his suits, sneakers and shoes. Renee' then worked on me saying "Meri, get ready for Tough Love. Going forward, you're not going to be modeling, so what do you need this dress and this jacket for?!"

We got rid of loads of this stuff, and were exhausted, but happy and moving on.

MOVE TO ROCKVILLE CENTRE

As I told Herb prior to moving into this apartment, we all live together. "It's you and your blood pressure and bp meter, and salt and Tic Tacs, and me and my diabetes and glucose-testing insulin pump and glucose supplies." But, having learned to keep my blood sugar higher rather than lower, I had this pretty well in control.

Packing and moving–loading and lifting boxes–was hard work. Herb was able. "How do you cut the packing tape without a pair of scissors?," he asked, marveling at my dexterity and creativity.

"My teeth," I shared. We laughed and together packed up.

PARKINSON'S DISEASE

I'd marked the cartons with rooms into which the cartons should go, and the movers and I and Herb placed these appropriately–or more or less appropriately. It was hard work, but we survived.

Our coop required that we carpet 75% of the floors. We shopped, debated colors, settling on a medium gray. Purchased, in a few days the store's men installed our wall-to-wall carpeting. We thought it looked beautiful–a field of gray–on the floors in our two bedroom/ two bathroom apartment.

From that point on, on our carpeted apartment floors, Herb could walk alone. But on advice of our physical therapist friend Aranka, Herb's bathroom needed carpeting, as well. Dear friend Marilyn and I cut the carpeting and installed it on Herb's bathroom floor, as well.

The fear was that Herb's blood pressure could drop, caused by sodium depletion in his blood, and thus, loss of balance and a fall.

While Herb's disabled Parkinson's disabled him, he still had the ability to play the mandolin. And, as I loved to sing, friend Marcia, the recreation director at a senior residence in Long Beach, invited us to join the group of seniors that performed there for their residents.

So every Thursday, I packed Herb's mandolin and my music I'd gathered and away I drove us–to Long Beach. With the group, about 6 seniors took our turns, the musical director accompanying us on the piano.

After the music, we all sat together and enjoyed the coffee and cookies provided by the residence, and enjoyed frolicking and telling jokes.

We could go outside. One day we walked to the post office. However, returning, across the street from our new home, Herb fell on the sidewalk. I could not lift him. Fortunately, some kind driver saw us, pulled over, got out and assisted Herb in sitting up.

I'd been carrying, in case of emergencies, salt tablets to raise Herb's blood pressure when needed. I pulled out some salt tablets and the Tic Tacs I also carried for after taste, and I gave this to Herb. Within about 20 minutes, Herb was improved.

The kind man offered to drive us to our home. But Herb believed he was strong enough, and I thought so, too. So we declined and thanked this gentleman for this offer. In a few more minutes, I held Herb's elbow, and we walked across the street and got home safely.

I determined that before leaving our home I would test Herb's blood pressure, and if low, or descending, I'd give him some extra salt tablets with Tic Tacs, for taste.

We'd go out to restaurants with family or friends. Several times he got low. Out of my pockets came my salt supplies and despite some initial resistance from my darling, into his mouth went the treatment. After the 20 minute wait time for the salt to metabolize, Herb improved.

You see, Herb was afraid of too much salt (sodium) causing a stroke. But, we'd learned that these small amounts could not cause a stroke. Also, several physicians told us, "Better that blood pressure be too high than too low."

In our new Rockville Center coop, for our entertainment, we'd meet friends for a movie, dance concert, a play or dinner. When Herb got low–and he did–out came the BP Meter and salts and Tic Tacs.

I learned how stubborn Herb was. After home dinners, at times, when Herb looked wobbly or sounded, with no alcohol, kind of drunk. I tried to get Herb to take the salt and Tic Tacs. But he resisted fiercely. I explained potential consequences and still, many times, Herb resisted. I phoned Jerry explaining the situation, and handed the phone to Jerry.

In his loving brotherly way, Jerry talked to Herb first about baseball or football, and when he relaxed a bit, Jerry told Herb: "Meri knows when you're bp is low and it would be correct to allow her to test you and, if necessary, if your bp were low, the few salt tablets and Tic Tacs will work and normalize your bp."

Herb accepted the salt tablets and Tic Tacs I offered, and in a little while he improved and could walk.

Through the end, two dementia tests proved negative. His brain worked fine.

We carried on: me and my diabetes supplies and Herb with his Parkinson's materials.

The neurologist had warned, "And you cannot drive, nor can you stand on the kitchen tiles without a supporting person." He wrote these on his business cards and gave them to me to post on our refrigerator, which is what I did.

Walking exercise was good for Herb and we could go outside. When Herb's legs were still strong enough to permit walking outdoors, I'd take him, holding onto the wheelchair. If he felt weak, he'd be able to sit down on this. I let Herb lead and together, we'd walk us around the parking lot. I also took Herb, with a wheelchair, to restaurants to meet family or friends.

We carried on: Herb and blood pressure meter, salt and Tic Tacs, and me with my insulin pump and glucose supplies.

SIS DEMENTIA AND DEATH

Many years and shows later, Sis was admitted to a Rehab Center.

Dementia, Freddie told me. I visited. Sis recognized me immediately. Her big smile lit the room, showing huge happiness. I helped my older sister to walk the corridor, Sis holding onto a wheelchair. We'd sing a few songs from our youths: "Too Young," "Only You,"and "Pretend". A few days later, she was released.

About three days later, Freddie phoned. Sis had passed away. She had refused to consult the physician who replaced her own doctor after he'd died. High blood pressure, Freddie explained.

I helped with funeral arrangements, said the eulogy. Grief, Freddie would need to deal with alone.

FRANK O'BRIEN, SINGING

I was now an experienced professional singer. My friend Judy who, like me, loved music, told me of a pianist/singer named Frank O'Brien. With his bassist Vinnie Ciarvolo, Frank headlined at local restaurants.

So, we found Cala Di Mare in Rockville Centre. Herb and I met Judy and her husband Len and dined, and enjoyed the terrific music. In between numbers, Judy mentioned to Frank that I sang and he invited me up. I went up, sang and felt like a star.

We followed Frank to many other restaurants. I always prepped a song or two, and had a wonderful time listening to, and making, music.

DESIRE TO MAINTAIN INDEPENDENCE

I understood that brave Herb wanted, for as long as possible, to be independent and not to burden me or even any aide.

I was now the family driver, chauffeuring us to doctor's appointments for each of us, taking us shopping for clothes for Herb and early on, to the supermarket.

Getting into our car, Herb would always plead, "Please, Mer, let me drive, You're sitting next to me. You can take my foot off the pedal and you can pull us over."

A few times I almost weakened. Thinking better, my heart breaking, I refused.

SWIMMING POOL

Herb and I had attended Echo Park's chlorinated swimming pool where we each enjoyed the pool. Herb used the low water walking lanes and I, my swim appliances supporting me, the deep lane in which I could tread, chat with other swimmers, and keep my eye on Herb. We each had fun and enjoyed good exercise.

I also took Herb to restaurants to meet friends.

Then Herb became less able to stand on his own and shower and change clothes. His disease was progressing.

AIDES

I spoke to my friend Marcia, a retired social worker. She advised, "You've got the long term care policies and Herb needs it, get it right away. Get 24/7 service."

We attended a Parkinson's Support group where Parkinson's patients shared their feelings, including fears. Social workers conducted this, and the topic of aides came up.

Many participants' families attended these monthly sessions. Many relatives volunteered that their aides made a world of difference.

Herb and I had this Long Term Care insurance and mentioned this. So Kathy, the chief social worker, spoke especially to us.

"If you have long term care, you should use it now. You've paid for it and Herb's condition is worsening. Start with three times a week, and when you need to you can increase the frequency. Many patients use it 24 hours a day. You've got it, and you need it, so why hold on to it!

Kathy continued, "I can talk to you privately, if you like. After this session, I'll call you, okay?"

We agreed.

Members and families had their piece of cake and coffee or tea at the session's end, and left.

Kathy called and reiterated her message, which sounded like the right thing to do. "Can I count on you to do this, Herb?" Kathy asked.

Realizing his declining situation, Herb answered, "I'll think about it. Give me some time."

I had previously checked with our financial advisor and he told me that, with our Long Term Care insurance and our investments, we can definitely afford this.

About a week later, sitting in the waiting room of my orthopedist's office, quietly, I asked Herb, "Are you ready to start the long term care?"

"Are you sure we can afford this? What will happen when you need care," said my ever-caring selfless husband. I don't want to take away our money from you when you need it."

"Herb, darling, I've spoken to Ed, our financial guy, and he said we had more than enough for both of us. So okay, you'll agree?"

"Yes, I do agree."

"Hallelujah," I thought. So I was determined and contacted this wonderful nursing care service I'd learned of from several people, and we began–first with 3 days progressing later to 24 hour care.

Aides came–some very good, others less good–but overall, they provided the care needed.

One night, Herb got himself out of the bed and fell. We took his pressure. It was low and we treated it.

Now we had to get a bed railing–and most importantly, increase our service to 24 hours/7 days a week.

One time in our apartment, between aide shifts, after lunch, Herb attempted to walk to the bathroom. Holding the back of his slacks, like he had an urgent call, he scooted along quickly like he needed the bathroom fast. I ran behind, trying to catch him if he fell.

Herb, unable to contain his movement and make it to his bathroom on time, collapsed on the carpet and dirtied it and part of the bathroom floor. Rubber gloves on, paper towels at the ready, I cleaned up all I could. The afternoon aide arrived in a while later and cleaned the remainder.

Herb had taken a few falls in the house. No major injuries on the carpeted floor. In time, despite Herb's refusal to use one, I bought him a walker.

Herb accepted the railing for the bed, and after a few more falls, he was pleased to hold onto the walker.

Even years before Herb 's Parkinson's diagnosis, I had some down mood swings. Herb wrote and handed me this message he'd typed on his computer:

Darling Merilee

This is just a short note to remind you that I LOVE you...just in case you forgot.

You are such a caring person and take-caring person. I am so grateful that you take good care of yourself and take such good care of your loving husband (me).

Please don't change, and forgive me for any bad things I may do.

LOVE,

Herb

Fourteen

LIVING

Herb had been an art teacher and calligrapher. Now, in our home, sitting at our dining table, he'd do puzzles, particularly crossword puzzles every morning, and paint on paper and with crayons I'd brought to the table.

He continued playing bridge, his brother driving them to senior centers.

With many of the aides, he played cards, his game of choice.

In nice weather, on Tuesdays when brother Jerry came to visit, we'd take Herb downstairs and bring him across the street to sit in a lovely little park.

These loving brothers would reminisce about sports, their families and Herb's Army career. You see that Parkinson's Disease depletes nerves and muscles throughout the body. They die. These conversations with Jerry were great because they got Herb to speak, strengthening his vocal chords, and to laugh about funny memories.

We bought him a smart television for the dining room/living room. In addition to his daily crossword puzzles, Herb watched baseball, football, old films, some Netflix films and many Johnny Carson re-runs, always chuckling at these.

And Seinfeld repeats. Whether before or after dinner–he loved these shows.

Many times he'd fall asleep watching, and that was alright.

January 16 seemed like a normal day. Herb's aides got him up, showered him and got breakfast on the table. He ate. Same with lunch. Herb played cards with the day-aide and watched tv. In the afternoon, aide Betty Lee gave Herb some arm exercises. His arms hurt him a bit–so he switched to some leg exercises.

His mood seemed slightly down, so I decided to pick up an Italian dinner which he'd always enjoyed: salad, veal parmigiana and rice pudding for dessert. Normally, Herb would want to down the complete portions. This evening he ate only about half and then went into the den to watch tv. At about 9pm, he was holding his arms.

"What's the matter," I asked.

"It hurts," he responded.

I got some pain ointment and applied it. No help.

"Will you take Tylenol, the pain killer?" I asked

On previous occasions he'd refused, This night, "Okay," he agreed. And I gave it to him.

He went to sleep, but at about 11 o'clock, he rose.

"What's the matter, Darling?"

I took his blood pressure and it was normal.

"My back hurts," he replied.

I knew that back pain could be an indicator of heart problems. "Okay, I told Herb and Edwin, Herb's evening aide. "Herbie, Dear, we're going to get you to the hospital."

And so Edwin put on Herb's slacks, jacket and hat, I donned my jacket and hat, and Edwin his. We sat Herb in his wheelchair and I drove us to the hospital's Emergency Room.

At check in, BP was normal. They took blood and we waited.

They gave him a hamburger for dinner. A few vegetables and some canned fruit. Herb could eat only some.

Finally blood work came back. "One of the cardiac enzymes was off. We've got to get you upstairs where cardiologists can work on you," we were told.

The resident in the ER told me, "They might have to insert a stent to clear an artery. Or, they might decide to treat your husband with meds."

They put Herb on a gurney. As the tech wheeled him away, I ran up to him. "I love you, Herb, Dearest, and Ed and I will pray for you," I told him.

No reply.

I watched Herb's balding head get smaller and smaller the closer to the elevator and farther away from me, they got.

The ER staff told us, "There's nothing you can do for him for now. Go home, get some rest and we'll call you."

Late that night I got a phone call. "It doesn't look good. Two stent tries didn't work. We think you should come over in the morning."

I called brother Jerry and shared this. He told me he'd gotten the same message. We said goodnight and that we'd see each other in the morning.

A PERFECT MORNING

This January 18 was a perfect morning. The sun was shining brightly, the cold weather–about 40 degrees–was tolerable. Herb, my darling husband of the past 50 years, died January 16 and would be buried this January 18 day.

For the past nine years, with my loving care and that of his nurses and aides, Herb coped with his Parkinson's Disease. I drove him to doctors appointments. We ate out with friends, when his legs could support him, and shared watching murder mysteries, war movies and comedy reruns, especially *Seinfeld* and the *Johnny Carson Show* on TV. He also enjoyed his card and game playing.

Prior to the day's event, to the funeral home, I'd brought the requested burial outfit: white shirt, jacket, red tie and trousers, socks and shoes. I'd also given the funeral parlor a deck of playing cards in a red box to bury with Herb (in case, I humorously conjectured, Herb was really alive and wanted to play solitaire.)

Herb used to love playing cards and knew all the games and had created two board games. He co-wrote a book on calligraphy with friend Geri. As a retired publicist, I booked Herb and Geri appearances on radio programs, a mention of his book in the Wall Street Journal and an interview on the syndicated *Joe Franklin TV Show*.

He'd play games and cards with his aides if they knew how, or he'd teach them. Rummy was a favorite.

I played with him and an aide at times. However, I'm not a game player, so I left Herb to play with his aide. Also, I had other things to do–shopping or filling out papers, as I did while I took care of my darling with his Parkinson's disease. I felt some guilt not sharing in his card-enjoyment–but duty called, as I was caring 24/7–and he was okay with this.

At the cemetery, at the funeral parlors car, their man got out of the hearse and asked me, "Would you like to see the body."

"Yes," I replied. "Definitely." Inside, on the coffin's white satin lining, Herb lay–eyes closed, appearing at peace.

He was dressed in his outfit, including the red tie, and I could see red sticking out of his shirt pocket. A closer look revealed the red playing card box. (I like to prepare clothes, but didn't plan this match.)

I told the funeral parlor's man, "Okay."

I wore a black sweater and black socks and allowing for my aging corns, wide width-shoes that fit my feet. Accessories: only a simple black-beaded hanging necklace and the 14 karat ring, black onyx with white dove, which, many years ago while in Venice, Herb bought for me.

My brother-in-law Jerry (Herb's brother), with wife Renee' at his side, picked me up and we went to the cemetery. I stopped at the bathroom, as did Renee', then we drove to the plot. Our nephew Sean arrived. He's an orthodox Jew and, at graveside, read special prayers, as he did at the hospital on the 16th before Herb died.

Rabbi Goren was already there and friends arrived soon. Marcia was there with her daughter Michele and son Seth. At each of their weddings, Herb had read their ketubah—a Jewish marriage contract, outlining the rights and responsibilities of the groom.

Friends Len and Judy—even older than Herb and I—were also there, as were our dear friend and co-author of the book Herb and Geri wrote, *Calligraphy in the Copperplate Style*. Geri made the long drive from her home in Monroe Township, New Jersey with her friend Jerry, to this cemetery in West Babylon, New York.

Herb and I were great friends with Geri and her husband Les and we'd frequently dine together. Years ago, we four took part in a cooking club, where members shared the fun of prepping and enjoying these dinners. About 17 years ago, Les sadly passed away.

It was wonderful seeing Geri. After the ceremony, lovingly, she told me. "You look well, Meri, but still anorexic. Why don't you try putting on some weight."

Standing towards the back of our friends, I saw Edwin Zulu, Herb's wonderful evening aide. A rotund Afro-American man, who, in addition to caring for Herb, helped me with household things–like setting up the stations on my boom box, or applying a paint to cover stains on my bathroom sink. I used to think of Edwin as a teddy bear and secretly wanted to hug him.

Edwin later told me that his wife was waiting in their car. At the end of the ceremony I went back to see her and thank her for coming. She got out and I hugged her and she hugged me back.

The rabbi performed the ceremony, kindly giving due personal points of Herb's beautiful character and life. Then he turned it over to me.

I'd always like to be ready, so about a year before, when not stressed, I wrote a eulogy, including Herb's military background and education. (Herb had been awarded, among many others, the Army's Sharpshooter Award.) This writing was detailed and I thought it was really good. However, for this real event, I could not locate the original. So I read the eulogy I'd written the night before, after which I closed my computer at 4 am.

This day, I wore no eye-make up, so, if I cried, makeup couldn't run. I didn't cry–just a little throat-choking, which swallowing fixed.

Jerry read his words, expressing all the love growing up Herb had shown him and the love he felt for his dear brother. He choked a bit, also relieved by swallowing, and some nose runs. His handkerchief took care of this.

Jerry and Herb Kaufman as children

Where were my tears for this precious man I loved with my whole body and soul?

Jerry and Renee' drove us home. I had a few hours till friends arrived for the shiva, the Jewish official period of mourning. Renee' suggested that we first stop at the supermarket for paper goods and drinks–water, sodas, coffee and several cakes and boxes of cookies.

Renee' and Jerry

From that time till the next day and a half our apartment was filled with friends, temple members and neighbors. Foods and candies filled their arms, then poured onto our tables.

Plentiful red hair neatly in place, Renee' was extraordinary at prepping– setting up the coffee and all the foods, which kept arriving. She would not let me do anything.

This was unlike nine years ago, when Herb and I moved in. For our "introduction to neighbors" wine party I'd adorned Herb with our host-apron with the little rose on the upper pocket. With a friendly smile on his face, Herb walked around serving guests glasses of wine or soda.

MERILEE KAUFMAN

Merilee, Jerry, Sean Kaufman and Herb

This day, my Herb, now gone, could no longer help me set out plates, utensils and cups–or smile for our guests. I was alone.

Jerry helped lots, acting a lot as host, as I wasn't supposed to do that, which was considered work. Also considered work was when the phone rang, as it did, I was not to pick it up (also work.) Jerry did. But I could talk after.

Loads of Herb's cousins called expressing condolences. And Sean was also so helpful where he could. From his Jewish organizations, he contacted several and one brought over additional tables.

Later, I spoke to my widowed friends, Geri, Marilyn (the Florida snowbird) and Marcia and asked, why had I yet shed no tears?

Each said, *in your own time.*

One day, alone in my apartment, sitting on my toilet I opened my cell phone to the photo gallery and saw the video from about a year before, of me and Herb dancing. My walls opened up. This happened several more times. Once tears were so great that my breathing was constricted–

just as asthma had done decades ago, when I breathed too hard. Quieting down, breathing normalized.

I looked through Herb's closet and found, in his portfolio, some calligraphy pieces he'd created. They were of famous sayings and prayers, like the one from Alcoholics Anonymous. The one that touched my heart was the poem by William Ernest Henly called *Invictus*. The last two lines I thought epitomized my brave unafraid Herb:

I am the master of my fate

I am the captain of my soul.

I decided to frame and prominently hang this, displaying Herb's magnificent calligraphy talent.

The framing store did a beautiful job. I'd selected a mahogany frame and a perfect gray matting, matching our carpet color, and a black trim. I paid $274 for the job and thought this was a lot of money. But, I figured, Herb was my one and only wonderful husband and this was worth every penny! I think artistic Herb would have approved of my selection.

In our apartment, I hung this on the living room wall and several times and stopped to admire it, realizing how talented Herb was. Naturally, at several of these early pauses, my tears-faucet again teemed . After some days, my crying stopped and I could comfortably sit on the living room couch and relax.

Six months after his death, it's a Herb-treasure I frequently enjoy,

Time has passed and I still love to perform and reap audience approval.

So much paperwork to wade through. It took several months to get through the grieving process and to allow myself to venture out into public and smile–my normal personality slowly returning.

Brother Jerry continues to visit Tuesdays–this time to console both for me and himself. We heal together.

At library courses, I resumed my love of writing poetry. Finally, at the Oceanside Library, a jam session was scheduled. I calendared it a month before and on session day, now 80 years old, I got all dressed up to look as good as I could. I coiffed my hair. But this time, no eye makeup, no lipstick. just a nice outfit I felt I'd look attractive in. With no amplifier or microphone–only my song lists and my voice, I entered the room.

Here I found two guitarists, about 15 years younger than me, strumming their strings and a seated lady watching. This woman, I later learned, had been a music teacher of one of the guitarists. I took out my lists of songs and sang songs I thought the musicians might know: *When the Red Red Robin Comes Bob-Bob Bobbin' Along*, *Don't Fence Me In* and *Pennies From Heaven*.. The guys accompanied with chords.

The two guitarists each selected and played songs of–their music–from the 60's and 70's, sung by Peter Paul and Mary, Billy Joel and James Taylor, to name but a few.

They also sang, when they remembered the words. I chimed in where I could, helping with lyrics I knew, and sometimes singing in my high range. I thought, if they like me, they like me. No one was judging. All thirsted for a good time.

After 45 minutes, the session had to end. The librarian asked if anyone minded if she shot photos for Facebook on social media and, no one objecting, she shot several.

Show-time completed, our musicians group exchanged phone numbers and e-mail addresses. The librarian mentioned that the library would probably program this again–in about a month and maybe keep it going every month, which made all of us very happy.

Unlike the old days, for this day's gig, with little formal preparation, I felt it went wonderfully. Knowing my songs and enjoying the music-making, I had a terrific time.

A few people had joined the room, increasing the audience number, and each came over to me and told me how much they enjoyed my singing. I left, merrily proceeding onto my errands and then home.

Compared to years ago, stepping onto the stage, I felt I was putting my life on the line, this day–having fun with the music informally, and making new friends–was so different.

The libraries offered writing courses and I attended and began writing poems.

Here are some, about my recent, and older, experiences:

IT...

...cannot be halted.

Herb, despite more than
a decade-long battle,
employing armaments:
exercise, puzzles,
music, dancing, art, TV,
laughing were he could,'
'
that victor slaughters my man.
Army triumphant –

undefeatable Death.

Loved ones grieve,
smile wanly
until the inevitable

chooses them.

EATING PIZZA

...your weekly treat
you were King.
Disciples took
a back seat to your
gustatory pleasure.
No one could
interfere. Ensconced
in your
wheelchair-throne,

unassisted, for
quarter of an hour,
all still
save for some
marinara and
mozzarella drippings.

"Some ice cream with a cookie-dessert,"
your mini-request.
This universe, yours.

Many pizza slices
and ice cream pops later,
you're gone. Still
always, you're
my King.

TO YOU
I'm beautiful, pretty
no more.

You can't help me

match eye make-up
choose an outfit that
hides any bulges,
whose color
doesn't flatter.

You had preferences,
but liked me in all, because
you loved me.

I WISH I COULD GIVE YOU...
...a beautiful package –
all the things you love:
bridge and gin rummy games,
crossword puzzles,
dinner with family...

spaghetti and beans,
veal marsala and potatoes,
carrot cake, an occasional beer.
good mysteries on tv
golf games, tennis,
good plays and films...

an outdoor walk: you, me,
aide at your side,
my hugs and kisses,
and you,

walking independently.

ALONE

MERILEE KAUFMAN

...in my home.
No company,
disturbances,
aides to supervise,
dinners to prepare...

no Herb.

Half a century
we were a couple –
a happy, beautiful,
loving team. Sharing,
helping each other.

We laughed, cried together,
enjoyed friends, restaurants,
each other's talents.

Uninvited,
time arrives.

Now, there's just
me,
free to read,
close my eyes,
cry, laugh, doze.
relax, be comfortable,
remember.
Be sad, happy, and be
at peace.

KISSES AND CARESSES

Spring is here.

VALLEYS AND MOUNTAINS

Tulips sport
coats red, pink.
To the sky
daffodils yawn
yellow petal arms

I'd drive us –
shopping to shows,
films to restaurants
to doctors.

From our driveway,
across Hall Street, we'd see
the crepe myrtle trees,
today still barren.
In our nine years here,
each July I'd point out
the trees
blushing lavender splendor.

I like the words "crept myrtle."
They're from a a song lyric
I used to sing
From the show "House of Flowers."

At home you filled in
the crossword puzzles,
played bridge, chess
mandolin, exercised.
Ate the meals I cooked
or brought in.
laughed at Seinfeld, and
YouTube's Johnny Carson reruns.

Like the seasonal tulips and daffodils
we, too, have our time

MERILEE KAUFMAN

This year I'll see the crepe myrtles
without you. Now I must
enjoy each sunrise, sunset.
good friends, foods, symphonies
alone, embraced only by
memories of
your kisses and caresses.

For my *What Now* feelings, I wrote:

MY WOODS

No sheets of snow, Mr. Frost –
and it's daylight –
not evening.
What shall I do?

My clock ticks on.
Seconds, minutes,
hours, days --
like petals from a flower
fly away.

Powder messages
sprayed from a plane.

What can I create–leave?

Fifteen

TEMPLE THRIFT SALE

I attended the Temple Avodah Sisterhood's semi-annual Thrift Sale today. Here, the Sisterhood sells new and slightly used clothes donated by congregants and local vendors. After nearly two weeks' of the Sisterhood's collection and setting out clothes in the temple's recreation annex, this beautiful fall Sunday, the sale was called for 9am which would go on till–to run through 3pm.

Monies collected benefit our temple and the needy in the neighborhood, and to medical organizations. This has been going on for nearly 20 years.

I attended, as I have in the past, to help sell, and also to pick up some warm hats and gloves for myself. I like bargains, and sale-prices are much cheaper than in department stores.

I collected and purchased my desired items, walked around the floor admiring the many and particularly admired many necklaces, bracelets and rings.

The dominant crowd, mostly female, thinned by noon, so I left to join friends for lunch. I followed this with a brief sojourn to my home to drop off my goods.

The Sisterhood, at 3pm, donated leftover goods to another charity whose truck calls for bagged items.

The whole room was jammed with tables full of shoes, sneakers, ties, suits, jackets, shirts, handbags, hats, blouses, socks, many separated for different age groups.

Perhaps due to my artsy background I leaned towards the dramatic in clothes.

I loved many of the necklaces on tables but didn't buy them because at 80 years old, I no longer dress up or find the need to and need to accessorize with crystal and big brassy jewelry.

However, on top of a cabinet, I spotted a woman's handbag. It was crafted in the "hobo-style" with fabric handles. I got this down and perused it closely. What really got me was the different fabrics that were sewn onto it–all over the bag. Multi-color swatches, about two inches in size, made of plaids, polka-dots, rectangles, triangles, and more, sewed one next to the other all over the bag.

I didn't need another bag, I told myself, so I put off the big decision, thinking I'll return at 3pm for the function's packing part–and if it wasn't yet sold, perhaps they'll give it to me.

Returning, that's what I did, inquiring right away, where was the bag which had been prominently displayed. "Susan," I was told, "had purchased it. And it was made in India."

It became more valuable to me and I felt like I was sliding down a mountain. I then planned to phone this "Susan" and offer twice what she paid for it. Unable to ascertain any further information–I gave up my current acquisition ambitions. Next time, I told myself, *buy it when I see it!*

It was 3pm and the packing was underway. All this merchandise was crammed in plastic bags, not leaving a single item on the temple tables.

Then, male temple members brought all the bags into the waiting truck.

Many of the congregants knew each other from the temple clubs and religious services. I knew some members and asked the names of many. We exchanged pleasantries andI said my hello's, asked directions for what I needed to know,

Afterwards, in the parking lot, I asked names of many of those I worked with, and got their "Rachel," "Paul," "Alans," "Jack," "Dora" and more. Along the way, they all asked for my name.

I felt included–like they wanted to know me in achieving. Toward our mutual goal of strengthening the temple., I felt like I was moving closer and making friends with these members. What I, or anyone, puts out, I realized, comes around to them.

MY 80TH BIRTHDAY PARTY

For a while, I felt depressed and down and discussed this with my internist, Dr. Simon. The first anti-depressant/anti-anxiety drug did nothing. Next call, Dr. Simon suggested I try another of these SSRI drugs. After three days my spirits lifted.

A friend suggested I attend writing workshops at local libraries. I did and returned to my poetry-writing.

I learned of a temple member who'd written a memoir. I read and enjoyed it. How about me writing a memoir, I wondered. And began.

One day, on my 80th birthday, with Marcia and another friend, all of us widows, went to lunch. I shared my existential concerns: I was now alone and the question was How should I live? What can I enjoy? Marcia, who in her younger years, was a party giver, suggested I make a birthday party.

It was an active move, and that's what I did. At a local diner, 13 friends, including Jerry and Renee', attended. What a wonderful event–seeing these friends, including Elaine Vipler, my friend from junior high school, and her husband Marvin! That was a special treat. And my usual dynamite standbys, too. I felt great intermingling with all.

MERILEE KAUFMAN

We all ate, chatted and had a superb time–especially, I think, me.

I began writing my memoir, many pieces of which got good reception in my workshop, and I got some good editing ideas. My interest in improving my writing grows.

Since the end of shiva, Herb's brother Jerry continues his weekly Tuesday visits, now just to me. This helps each of us heal.

My diabetes of 65 years duration is now taking its toll. Neuropathy gives me pains in my legs. However, I can still see, feel, hear, smell, taste and exercise. And Tylenol helps some. I can also still enjoy theater, food, music and people.

I thank God for my life: my mother, father and sister and wish I could have told them all the love and gratitude for them I feel today. Each did their best, I know.

My writing will continue, and strong, I will face whatever fate brings me next.

Thank you for taking the time to read this.
Merilee Kaufman

Postscript

CHRISTMAS EVE

"What are you doing Christmas eve?" asked Carlos, the husband of Lilliana. They're the couple who clean my apartment every two weeks.

"Nothing. I'll be here by myself."

"Oh, by yourself!," replied Carlos, a note of shock and sadness in his voice. "Christmas eve, you shouldn't be alone!" And as he said this, he turned to Lilliana who was already out the door. Quietly he related this, she nodded, then he returned.

"You must come to our family gathering at my sister's house.

My face must have held questions.

"It's not far from here–just in Freeport. He and Lilliana, who'd just rejoined us, kept saying. "Do come! We'll pick you up and bring you home. And you can be with our family. Because now, you're part of our family–and no one should be alone Christmas eve.

They were referring to the fact that I was alone since my husband Herb passed away last January.

To go or not go–that was my conflict.

I decided to join them, to not too distant Freeport, "I can drive there," I told them.

Lilliana jumped in and said, "No, we'll call for you. About 8, okay?"

"Okay," I agreed, then immediately thought of what I could bring them–and what I might wear.

Discussing the gift problem, friends suggested money would be the best. They could buy what's best for them. So that was decided. The what to wear question: closer to the date, I'd decide when I learned the weather outlook.

On December 23, learning the weather prediction, I selected dark green leggings and a red sweater top and a slightly glittery necklace with red and crystal beads and a pendant with a red stone on a silver backing. This was from my entertaining days.

I was early, so I read my new mystery by Michael Connelly.

Time to go. I put on my light weight jacket, 180 earmuffs and gloves and waited downstairs.

A few minutes later, Lilliana pulled up, with daughter Valentina inside.

They were so happy to see me, as I was to see them.

It was 8pm and dark outside, and we proceeded, Lilliana, at times, talking on her cell phone, which made me nervous. Happily we arrived.

Up the steps we were greeted by their barking dog, Frisky, then all the family–except Carlos. He was coming later I was told.

I was welcomed by Carlos' brother-in-law, also named Carlos, and his wife, Claudia, Carlos' sister, and two other Carloses. They were all happily engaged. In the small living room, I sat and chatted with Claudia, Carlos' sister, while the younger set gathered in the dining room and spoke, mostly in Spanish. They invited me to join, but it seemed they all knew what they were discussing–which, due to my minimal knowledge of Spanish, was out of my grasp.

Valentina put one of their TV platforms on softly, and Josh Groban sang Christmas songs.

So, again, I was alone, though surrounded by loving people.

Finally, "Dinner is here," I heard, and Carlos, Claudia's husband, went to the car to bring it in. I saw cartons carried by this Carlos, and Carlos, the older son carry the food up.

I still smelled nothing like home cooking in the oven. Finally, Claudia heated the aluminum trays in the oven and the rooms released the fragrance of FOOD.

I realized that these people brought in meals, at least on this night, it appeared, rather than cooked.

Carlos, Lilliana's husband arrived. "Does Claudia cook?" I asked him.

"Oh, yes, and she's a very good cook."

I walked into the dining room and perused the platters. On them were shrimp, chicken, corn cobs, rice and bread–and ribs. Again, Lilliana invited me, "Won't you have some?"

"I had my dinner at home, but thanks so much, Lilliana."

Alone, in the living room, I watched tv and thought, I could be in my own home reading or watching tv. But I gazed at the family's beautifully decorated tree. Family members, dinners complete, trickled into the living room, and sat down.

Carlos had told me about nephew Carlos' interest in performing theatre. Proud mother Claudia had shown me on video the morning's church production, in which Carlos and Valentina sang and acted their lead parts. I told Carlos that I'd worked administratively in theatre and saw what a difficult road it is–with shows coming in and closing.

"I want to be on Broadway," he told me, a swagger in his voice.

Lilliana mentioned to the group that I sing, and asked me to sing. So I performed some Christmas songs, and all applauded, many telling me what a beautiful voice I had. I thanked them and was glad I could add something to the festivities.

I'd asked Carlos what time does the family open the many Christmas presents beneath the tree. "About 12." However, earlier he'd told me he'd take me home whenever I wanted.

Seemed like now was a good time and I told him. I got my jacket and Carlos helped me put it on. I went over to the group. "Thank you for inviting me to join your wonderful family. It's been a total pleasure and I wish you all a very Merry Christmas." And I turned to leave.

"No, no, the group all called. We've got something for you."

I walked toward the two small Christmas shopping bags Valentina held out for me. Surprise gripped my face and I smiled.

"Thank you so much," I said, hoping Lilliana had given the group the money Christmas present I'd given her to give to hostess Claudia.

Carlos ahead of me, I went down the stairs and entered his car.

Driving home, Carlos mentioned that tomorrow, Christmas Day, he had to work about 4 hours. I realized his work load and tried to lighten it, offering "More work, more money," to which he agreed.

I suggested, "You must have a wonderful mother." "I do," he offered, "and she's still alive in El Salvador, at 75 years old, still doing good things. When she was younger, without medical training, she used to deliver 10 babies in a week. People came to her because they knew she cared and could do the job."

"You're lucky," I told him. And by that time we were at my home. Carlos got out and asked if I wanted him to accompany me upstairs. I declined, but gave him a warm hug.

Carlos waited till I got my key in the door. Then we wished each other Merry Christmas.

Reaching my apartment I looked in each bag. One held a big yellow citrus flavored lemon candle. The other bag was filled with a small photo frame, a box containing rub-in hand ointment and two singly wrapped Ghirardelli chocolates.

I'll put all away in the morning, I told myself, and just kept thinking–not necessarily of the gifts, but of the warmth, and belonging, I got from that evening, being a part of that wonderful family.

Afterword

CONDOLENCE NOTES RECEIVED ON HERB'S PASSING:

From neurologist Dr. Joseph Jeret:

Dear Merilee, I'm terribly sorry for your loss. Herb dealt so well with the highs and loads of Parkinsons Disease.

In the 10 years I've treated him, with your support, Herb has been diligent, pursuing treatment and following directions. I'm proud to have known such an intelligent and cooperative patient.

And Merilee, you have been the best of caretakers I've known in my practice. Your attention, sensitivity and caring are to be admired.

And brother Jerry, you've been exceptional, loving and caring, as well.

I'm pleased to have known your wonderful family.

-Dr. Joseph Jeret and Cathy and Bianca

From internist William Simon:

AFTERWORD

Dear Merilee,

I'm so sorry for your loss. Herb was a brilliant patient and person.

This showed up, I could see, during his visits: in courteous interacting with me and love of you, his wife.

Sincerely, Dr. William Simon and Staff

To leave on an up note: A colleague from one of my writing workshops wrote this on a beautiful decorated parchment paper:

ODE TO MERILEE
With tons of talent, completely unique,
Her life is one long creative streak.

Poetry! Music! There isn't an art
She hasn't explored with her soul and her heart.

Now as she embarks on this next phase,
A whole new trail for her to blaze,

So strong, so smart, and still co cute!
Marvelous Merilee has earned a tribute.

Odes are made by friends like me
But only God could make Merilee!

Acknowledgments

"Special thanks to my wonderful editor, Katherine Abraham and publisher, Stephanie Larkin, both for selecting my book, and for offering valuable fixes editorially, and praises. I hold all dearly.

I'm especially grateful to my dear friend (also Herb's cousin) Sandy. This accomplished novelist praised the value of workshops. She read my early drafts and kept encouraging me to write.

I'm so grateful for libraries, especially their writing workshops and leaders who inspire and encourage.

Merilee Kaufman

About the Author

Award-winning writer/poet/actress/vocalist Merilee Kaufman has been called a Renaissance woman of her time. Merilee has sung in clubs, libraries and residences across Long Island. Written works by this award-winning poet have appeared in numerous publications including *The New York Times* and the anthology *Sarah's Daughters Sing*. Mrs. Kaufman is listed in the *American Directory of Poets and Short Story Writers* and has been a member of both The Poetry Society of America and Poet's House.

Merilee attended the High School of Performing Arts in New York City and attended acting classes with Warren Robertson in his Acting

Workshop, and at New York's Herbert Berghof Studio, where she studied singing technique with George Taros.

Mrs. Kaufman has performed in numerous community theater productions and with her duo, *Ivories and Melodies*, presented musical presentations of standards songs. With a writing partner she acted in original plays, also presenting readings of original poetry, essays and articles.

She has been featured in articles in *The New York Times, Newsday and the Oceanside Herald*. The author has been a guest on the syndicated Joe Franklin TV Show, The Morning Show on WABC-TV and the Joan Hamburg Radio Show on WOR Radio.

This creative force lives in Rockville Centre, New York.

Several years ago, this multi-talented lady retired from running her successful public relations firm. She currently resides in Rockville Centre.

www.ingramcontent.com/pod-product-compliance
Lightning Source LLC
Chambersburg PA
CBHW061737070526
44585CB00024B/2715